CLOSER EVERY YEAR THE STORY OF

TRAVIS

Published in 2000 by
INDEPENDENT MUSIC PRESS LTD.

Closer Every Year - The Story of Travis
by Mike Black

British Library Cataloguing-in-Publication Data.
A catalogue for this book is available from The British Library.

ISBN 1-89-7783-19-1

Every effort has been made to contact the photographers whose
work has been used in this book - however a few were unobtainable.
The publishers would be grateful if those concerned would contact
Independent Music Press Ltd.

Cover & book design by Phil Gambrill.

Picture Credits:
6: Andy Willsher/SIN; 10: Mel Cox/SIN; 19: Angela Lubrano/Live;
22: Andy Willsher/SIN; 29: Angela Lubrano/Live; 33: Justin Thomas/All Action;
36: Suzan Moore/All Action; 41: REX Features; 45: Steve Gillet/Live; 48: Angela Lubrano/Live;
53: Justin Thomas/All Action; 56: Simon Meaker/All Action; 59: Suzan Moore/All Action;
62: Suzan Moore/All Action; 67: Ellis O'Brien/All Action; 73: Andy Willsher/SIN;
78: Rob Hann/Retna; 85: Angela Lubrano/Live; 88: Martyn Goodacre/Retna;
95: Sue Moore/All Action; 100: Rob Hann/Retna; 107: Rob Hann/Retna;
115: Angela Lubrano/Live; 120: Martyn Goodacre/Retna; 129: Roy Tee/SIN

Cover Image: Rob Hann/Retna

Colour Plates: Sue Moore/All Action; Gilbert Blecken/SIN; Melanie Cox/SIN; Justin Thomas/All Action;
SueMoore/All Action; Roy Tee/Sin; Ian Yates/Retna; Soulla Petrou/Retna

INDEPENDENT MUSIC PRESS
P.O. Box 14691
London
SE1 3ZJ

Web www.impbooks.com
e-mail info.imp@virgin.net
Fax 020 7357 8608

CLOSER EVERY YEAR THE STORY OF

TRAVIS

BY
MIKE BLACK

INDEPENDENT MUSIC PRESS
LONDON

CONTENTS

CHAPTER ONE

MILLENNIUM MEN

John Lennon, Keith Richards, Bryan Ferry, Ron Wood, Graham Coxon, Freddie Mercury... find the common denominator. The answer is art school. There's no reason why those gifted in the visual arts shouldn't turn to music, and the student's life offers plenty of time to meet like-minded people and form a band. Few bands, though, can boast three former art students...

Yet the music produced by Travis, namely Fran Healy, Andy Dunlop and Dougie Payne, along with fourth member Neil Primrose, is as non-élitist as they come. Okay, Fran dropped out after a tutor insisted he wouldn't hang one of his paintings – a naked body with a cartoon head, entitled 'Some Mothers Do Have 'Em' – on a wall; so he went off and wrote songs instead which have ended up in millions of households worldwide.

Such was Travis's dominance of the British music scene as 1999 ended that as 2000 began, *The Man Who* celebrated its 33rd week in the listings. Travis had become important to a large constituency ever since the release of this superb second album in May 1999. Whereas its predecessor, *Good Feeling*, had followed the standard 'indie bad' pattern of entering the charts at its highest position then plummeting as general indifference took hold, *The Man Who* proved through a combination of strong singles, a string of triumphant festival appearances over the summer and the lack of significant new rock releases in the autumn to retain a stranglehold over a Top 5 chart position.

The consequence was that Travis fans ranged from 15 to 50, their Scots pop-rock hitting a universal chord with different generations. And when the art-school mentality kicked in again, in the shape of a co-ordinated visual campaign that encompassed single and album covers and videos, Travis suddenly seemed to be much more than the sum of its parts. It was all a long way from the dingy room over a Glasgow bar that had contained them, their hopes and dreams, as recently as 1996...

There used to be a rock television programme called the *Old Grey Whistle Test* that owed its name to the theory that a record would be a hit only if its tune was so memorable that the 'old greys' (music publishing commissionaires) could whistle it. Fran Healy invented the modern equivalent when he did a demo of 'Why Does It Always Rain On Me?', the song that broke Travis to a worldwide audience. He told a taxi driver, while making conversation, that he was in a band called Travis. 'He'd never heard of us, and asked what we sounded like, so I gave him the demo and he played it. At the end of the song he just went "That's the story of my life, son." I knew then that this single was something special.'

Travis are indeed all things to all men (and women). The very first cover story on them had come from the gay magazine *Boyz*, one of whose questions had been 'When you're on stage, do you notice boys in the audience touching themselves?' Then there was the letter from 'Gordon of Chester' to another gay mag that stated 'I'd strum

Fran's guitar any day of the week'. The singer's attitude to being a gay pin-up? 'It's great!'

Whatever musical flavours they chose to serve up in the future to their now sizeable fan following, the band had long since transcended the 'indie' bracket they'd quite understandably occupied when they first came on the scene. And Fran Healy saw few limits to his ambitions. 'I'd say I wanted to sell about 10 million albums.'

'The ideal situation would be to make absolute fuckloads of money doing this and then not ever worrying about having to get a shitty job.'

As to the future, the man memorably described by one besotted critic as combining 'the Bambi-boy looks of a *Just 17* pin-up and a voice that revs between catch-in-the-throat confessional and full-blown, guttural roar,' was, before *The Man Who* hit gold, still looking at the life he'd escaped. 'The ideal situation would be to make absolute fuckloads of money doing this and then not ever worrying about having to get a shitty job. Because I just don't want to do that.' Somehow one doubts he has to worry now...

At the end of the day, if Travis stand for anything, it is the glory and the mundanity of regular people with regular lives. This is their story...

I ♥ FRID
A CUDDLE
I ♥ EATING
YOU
TO DANCE
POP
I ♥ FRID
ROCK N ROLL
A CUDDLE

CHAPTER TWO

EARLY DAYS

Occasional kilt-wearing Celt, Francis Healy, was actually born several hundred miles away from Bonnie Scotland, in the Midlands town of Stafford, on 23 July 1973. He was an only child, his mother Marion bringing him back to Glasgow when her marriage broke up a year after he was born. Fran has since been typically blunt about this childhood instability: 'I am the result of a shite relationship.'

His mum took a part-time job in a bank to make ends meet and, having moved back to her childhood home in the suburb of Cathcart, shared the upbringing of the only child with her parents. Fran recalls his grandfather entertaining him from an early age with poems and pictures, while several other members of the family showed real artistic talent, although this would remain largely untapped.

At age five, Fran proudly told his mum he was going to be a star - two years later he started out on that long haul by winning a competition for singing Scottish songs. 'It was the first time I got on a stage,' he'd later recall with pride. 'They put a kilt on me, I sang a song called 'Westering Home' and won a certificate.' When he was little, singing was part of his everyday life - indeed, when he used to forget his house number, his mum used to tell him to sing it... 'So I used to go home singing, "Two-three-seven"!'

For a man who admits he can be overcome by waves of melancholy, there were tales of tragedy in the family history: his mother's elder brother drowned in the Forth and Clyde canal, aged just nine, and his aunt could have been a 'brilliant artist', but she drowned too. Another uncle was run over by a horse and cart. Why does it always rain on me? Quite...

'They put a kilt on me, I sang a song called 'Westering Home' and won a certificate.'

He saw his father, long-distance lorry driver Frank Healy, infrequently, the most recent time in 1983 at the first communion of his half-brother Ryan. The relations he saw more often were a close-knit bunch, often going on holidays to the seaside in a minibus when Fran was just knee high. A later trip in 1985 was to Blackpool, and he's still got a group shot of Uncle Bill, Auntie Chrissie, his mum and his cousin on the prom. It was the summer Boris Becker won Wimbledon as an unseeded teenager and Live Aid rocked the world; Fran watched half of this legendary event in Blackpool and the finale once safely back at home. Fran has described his attraction to music as its ability to soundtrack people's lives - strangely, the song that associated itself with this particular seaside outing was ancient Eurovision winner 'Save All Your Kisses For Me', by the

Brotherhood of Man. Even after all these years, he confesses to being word perfect!

Though Fran's three best pals now are all male, he admits to being more comfortable in female company. 'All kids should be brought up just by their mums,' he remarks. 'I don't think men can do it. I'd love to be a father, but I might not be interested like most guys. Dougie's got three sisters, and it makes you think about things very differently. There's definitely a feminine aspect to my songs. A tenderer side.'

Fran bought records very rarely, and despite the financial rewards of Travis's latter-day success, that's still the case. To this day he listens to the radio more than his own CD collection, and this is usually where he finds his inspiration. One early favourite was Madonna, his first ever pop-star crush. 'I'm not sure what it was... er... a sexual awakening. I thought she was fantastic. When she sang 'Like A Virgin', I wasn't thinking Virgin, I was thinking Virgin Mary.'

Madonna also provided the soundtrack for when he fell in the first time, also in the eventful summer of '85. 'I saw this girl across a crowded little boat. We were going on a cruise through Scarborough and I saw this girl, Catrina Burns, who'd always been in our class at school, but suddenly she had a light around her. Anyway, she told me to "eff off." I remember lying on my bed crying, listening to 'Crazy For You'... ' The story did, however, have a happy ending. 'It was one of the first times in my life when I was like, "That person, I'm gonna have her no matter what!" And it was true! I got her in the end. We got each other.'

The first single he bought, Adam Ant's 'Prince Charming', from four years earlier, had caught his eye as much for the Advent Calendar-style packaging as the tribal drumbeat of the music. People in his school class used to steal the chalk from the classroom blackboard to emulate Ant's face paint. Fran wasn't actually a big fan of the music, but rather bought the record because of the peer pressure: 'Everyone was talking about how good it was, so I felt I had to buy it.'

School wasn't a pleasant experience for Fran Healy; he was picked on at primary school, though he denies this was anything to do with the fact that his father wasn't around. One of his worst persecutors has since died of a heroin overdose, and he admits to having gained a perverse satisfaction from hearing that news. Back in the 1980s, instead of retreating into his schoolboy shell, Fran tried to work out what made the popular kids popular, and took his lead from a classmate called Paul 'who was good looking, sparkling and the big kids loved him.' He made the effort to become more popular and outgoing, and it worked – hence, perhaps, his mixture of effervescence and vulnerability as a musician.

'I walked around as if I had a huge neon light that said "weird"... they used to follow me home and beat me up.'

There have been flashbacks to this period in Fran's later work, notably the clever refrain in the chorus of 'Writing To Reach You'. 'It's a feeling I got when I was bullied at school this funny sensation like my legs were crossing, like I was turning inside out. And I still get that whenever I'm feeling threatened. My eyes swop, my ears swop, everything feels the wrong way round.'

As an only child, Fran didn't have the luxury of elder siblings willing to mete out summary justice on their brother's behalf. Despite looking the same as everyone else, he continually found himself the target of bullies and had to fight his own battles. 'I walked around as if I had a huge neon light that said "weird"... they used to follow me home and beat me up.'

The day Fran exorcised his demons came at age 14 when he took on the biggest neighbourhood bully. Perhaps tellingly, it was when his adversary spat in his face that he 'went mental', found hitherto unsuspected inner reserves of strength and 'kicked the shit out of him.' Interestingly, when Travis won a *Q* award in late 1999, Fran revealed to Radio 1 listeners that he'd won a trophy for his skills in karate 'when I was a wee guy... it was like the proudest thing I've ever done.'

Perhaps surprisingly for a nascent lyricist, reading took a back seat to television in Fran's life, as he struggled to enjoy the first five pages of most books that were recommended to him. There were no books lying around the house nor even, for a while, a record player: snatched glances at his mother's *Daily Mirror* combined with the box to give young Fran his life insights. The first book he did read from cover to cover, at age 11, had a profound effect on him. It was Sue Townsend's *The Secret Diary Of Adrian Mole* after which Fran began a journal of his very own. Drawing, too, connected with him in a way the written word had not, and he began to formulate ideas for an art-centred career. Though he admits he's no Picasso, he still harbours the ambition 'to do and sell paintings.'

The role of radio remained crucial to introducing new music to Fran's life, and getting his own on the airwaves became a dream. 'Radio's important,' he confirms. 'It's free, and it's everywhere, so people can hear your music without choosing it – and if it stays in their heads then it's worked.'

One song that made a deep impression when it came over the airwaves in 1988 was 'Need You Tonight', a slice of Rolling Stones-style funk-rock by Australian band INXS. In view of Travis's later exploits, they were an unlikely group for Fran to adopt as his own, but he was mightily impressed by singer Michael Hutchence. A friend introduced him to Hutchence's other albums, and he became a confirmed fan.

When Hutchence killed himself in November 1997, the Travis singer would compose a eulogy in 'High As A Kite', the title of which reflected his status as much as his drug habits. Despite this admiration, Fran denies he ever really idolised anybody: 'I've never had a hero.'

Fran had enjoyed his first taste of live music in late 1986 courtesy of a friend, Brian Butler, who won tickets in a raffle to see one-hit wonder Owen Paul at the Pavilion Theatre in Glasgow. The twelve-year-old Fran and friend were the only two guys in the audience and were taken aback by the crowd response: 'It was an amazing gig, it was just mental... kids screaming and going totally apeshit. It didn't really matter what was happening on stage. I just remember going, "This is amazing! This is totally top!", not thinking, "God, I'd love to do this."'

As previously mentioned, television was a staple part of the entertainment diet at the Healy household, and it was during an episode of the American sitcom *Cheers* that a nugget of inspiration first planted itself in Fran's mind. The character Norm was talking to a friend about how he overheard his boss saying he was going to get rid of all the driftwood. Although Fran was only twelve, the notion of people being called driftwood stuck in his head. 'I think it was my first experience of a metaphor.' One that would take several years to bob back to the surface...

Fran's pop dreams really started to take flight at the age of 14, when his mum bought him his first guitar, an Encore acoustic, for Christmas. The catalyst was nothing less than a legend, and one of the rare performers who could speak to both Fran's generation and his mother's – Roy Orbison, who was guesting on *The Jonathan Ross Show* in what would be one of his last performances before he died of a heart attack in late 1988. Often known as the Big O, Orbison stormed to fame in the early 1960s through a combination of a quavering, tremulous and utterly unique voice, a swarthy, saturnine image accentuated by dark glasses and the respect of the beat generation that seemed to be washing away most other solo stars.

Fran's first tentative stage steps were taken while still at school with a band called Strange Relationship, which swiftly gave way to the Sun Gods (who, according to the singer, are still going but are now called Bulb Chutney). Trivia freaks may care to note their bass player, Jamie O'Donnell, went on to play with Bobby Gillespie in Spirea X, making the Sun Gods a footnote in not one but two future Rock Family Trees.

'His singing was okay but nothing spectacular, although he did a mean Mick Jagger impression with 'Sympathy For The Devil.'

'I can tell you Fran's voice has improved enormously from those days,' says school friend Robert Elliott, who was tracked down by the excellent Travis website *As They Are*. He remembers seeing his classmate performing in the school assembly hall with the Sun Gods. 'His singing was okay but nothing spectacular, although he did a mean Mick Jagger impression with 'Sympathy For The Devil.''

While Fran was no slouch academically, and was gifted enough to qualify for art school, music would prove to be the one thing that he'd stick at, overcoming his Jagger fixation to forge an identity of his own. Looking back on his upbringing, Fran credits his mother for giving him 'a boxer's attitude', namely the persistence to take the repeated knocks, but also acknowledges this has been made easier in the company of his three friends...

Drummer-to-be Neil Primrose, the eldest member of Travis by some 24 days, was born on 20 February 1972 in Cumbernauld, one of Glasgow's satellite 'new towns'. Not that he was to see too much of it; his father was a power station engineer, so the family was always on the move wherever the job took him. A posting to

Middlesborough was followed by a series of moves across the north-east of England that spanned the first ten years of Neil's life, with the sad result that Neil had to make new friends – or enemies – wherever he went. 'I basically got the shit kicked out of me,' the perennial new boy once reflected.

Returning to Glasgow, he made friends with a lad called Ronnie who played the drum in an Orange marching band. Thankfully, it was the musical side of this pastime and none of the sectarianism for which Scotland is sadly renowned that rubbed off. His other passion was swimming, the 200 metre butterfly stroke being his speciality; while a teenager he made it into the national C Class – 'one down from being able to swim for Scotland. I suppose if I'd stuck it out for another year, I might've got somewhere.'

Instead, the fledgling drummer answered an advert in a local shop window by a cabaret band looking for a percussionist. It was in the ranks of this act, Running Red, that he first met guitarist Andy Dunlop. Andy joined from heads-down thrash band the Flumps and although he insists they were dreadful, Neil still enjoyed it more than his day job in the stockroom at Glasgow shoe emporium Schuh.

Neil had plenty of musical influences to draw on, his parents 'bohemian' record collection being full of the sounds of the 1960s. Indeed, Neil drew on them so deeply that, by the start of the 1980s, he'd been a fully paid-up member of the Walker Brothers fan club and wondering why his schoolmates were not!

His later revered dedication to drumming was evident early on, although perhaps the most famous example was during the 1996 World Cup. After breaking his leg in an impromptu game between band and roadies, he was wheeled on stage a few days later, with his leg sticking from behind his kit in a plaster cast. According to Fran, 'You could chop his arms off and his head off and he'd still want to go up and play.'

Neil might have gravitated towards the drums as his instrument of choice, but he wanted to sing too. Fortunately he found a role model in his parents' LP collection - his choice was Levon Helm, the all-singing, all-drumming fulcrum of The Band. Little did a teenage Neil know that, one decade on from his drumming debut, he'd be recording in The Band's home village of Woodstock...

Two of his future bandmates, the aforementioned Andy Dunlop and Dougie Payne, were born the same year as him – both in Glasgow on 16 March and 14 November respectively, and both the

sons of bank managers. Dougie's earliest memory of life in the upper middle-class south side of the city is falling off a wall into a rose bush at the age of three. His first major artistic triumph *en route* to art school came not long afterwards when he won a local paper's colouring competition. The prize, a crisp £5 note, was riches indeed: he was amazed his father couldn't retire on the strength of it! Instead Dad took him to buy a dart board, and a love of the 'arrows' has endured to the extent that there's been a board in every house or flat he's lived in since.

Musically, Scots teen sensations the Bay City Rollers provided him with his first musical memory courtesy of two older sisters who insisted he perform their 1975 chart-topper 'Bye Bye Baby' for them. He's rather more grateful that one of those siblings, Gill, played him David Bowie's *Hunky Dory* album from the age of six upwards; 'I was immediately smitten', he admits, adding that he'd buy albums on CD by the Beatles and Bowie years later and wonder how it was he already knew the words! (Interestingly Fran can't bear Bowie, whose music conjures up pictures of 'him dancing around in a leotard.')

Clearly, growing up in a family with musical taste proved no hindrance to Dougie's ambitions, though until he was invited to join Travis he'd never so much as picked up a bass guitar in his life let alone played with a band! He was also a big reader, with the Adrian Mole book that had so inspired Fran a favourite of his, too. Dougie was a keen boy scout and was 'proficient in all camping skills. I remember skinning rabbits and sticking skewers up their bottom when we had to survive out in the night.'

Such life skills may have turned Dougie on to the life of a 'total backwoodsman' – but though he was once a member of pre-Cubs organisation the Beavers ('because they had such a great name') all Andy Dunlop wanted to do when he grew up was rock! He admits his record collection ran the gamut of metal, from Australian giants AC/DC (a particular favourite) to ZZ Top.

Born on 16 March 1972, Andy grew up in Lenzie, some 15 miles north of Glasgow. It was a peaceful suburb... until he started two years of piano lessons and took up the guitar. Perhaps it was the fact that AC/DC's diminutive guitarist Angus Young played atop his bandmate brother's shoulders wearing full school uniform that inspired the once shy, bespectacled Andy to pick up the instrument. But when he was enticed up on stage to take part in a talent contest at a *Radio 1 Roadshow* – one of British youth's summer rituals for fully two decades now – it wasn't 'Whole Lotta Rosie' that he decided to play but the theme for TV funny man Benny Hill. '… Rosie' could hardly have proved less popular, since he was beaten by a boy playing his *armpit*…

He'd have his revenge in the summer of 1999, when Travis were summoned to strum at Newquay, Cornwall, on the lawns of the Headland Hotel. ironically, the guitar he strummed – though considerably more expensive than the one youthful Andy had played that day – was unplugged, as the group were miming.

So there you have it, four ordinary lads all linked by their Glaswegian roots and a love of rock music. The city, of course, is a hotbed of musical activity with venues ranging from the small to the large. Best example of the former was King Tut's Wah-Wah Hut, the basement of a terraced house that has gone down in history as the venue where Oasis were first spotted by Alan McGee. The first step on the stardom ladder for many a local band, Barrowlands Ballroom, was the other end of the scale, 'the best venue in the UK' in Fran's estimation and a holy grail where only the biggest acts played.

Each future member of Travis had separately enjoyed their own initiation to the unique atmosphere there: Andy had seen Erasure, while his future bandmates had all gone for home-grown heroes: Fran the sophisticated agit-pop of Hue and Cry, Neil those blustering, bagpipe-guitar merchants Big Country and Dougie a potent double bill of Love and Money supported by a Texas still many years from their current multi-platinum status.

As musical dreams remained tantalisingly out of reach, any of the quartet would gladly have settled for an outing at King Tut's. Little did they realise they'd make it all the way to the biggest hall of all…

CHAPTER THREE

ART-SCHOOL HEROES

Fran, Dougie and Andy first met in 1991 as fellow students at the Glasgow School of Art. Fran studied painting and Dougie sculpture, while Andy was training to be a goldsmith. Within its hallowed halls, the trio attempted to create enough works of art to gain their degrees – Dougie and Andy both finished their courses, while Fran dropped out. 'One of the things that made it easier,' he grimaces, 'was when one of my tutors said about a painting of mine, "I'm not putting that on the fucking wall." I remember thinking, "This is an art school, you're allowed to do anything you like"… '

That said, he believes it taught him an important lesson in life. 'One of the best things for me about going to art school,' he later expounded, 'was realising that you've got to actually *want* to do something. Being good at doing something is not even half the battle.'

'I had big problems with painting,' he continues. 'I could never finish a painting. I never knew when it was finished. I don't have this problem with songwriting. I can write a song and then it's there. Ready, complete without anyone ever changing a word or a sentence. That gives me so much satisfaction." This creative openness and simplicity is perhaps at the very core of what makes Travis's songs so appealing to so many.

Dougie and Andy met on their very first day, discovering a mutual affection for cheap lager and 1960s throwbacks the Monkees. Though they didn't realise it then, their bank manager fathers were long-lost friends who lost touch. Dougie: 'My dad and Andy's dad used to know each other, like, 40 years ago. Used to go for lunch together. They lost touch and had no idea at all, and then we reunited them at a show where we were supporting Beth Orton. It was like, 'George!' 'Peter!'"

Dougie and Fran had encountered each other at a life drawing class, when Dougie did a fantastic Rolf Harris impression while he was sketching - 'We've been best mates ever since.'

Sculptor-to-be Dougie used to call his goldsmith pal 'Elfie' instead of Andy due to his habit of 'sitting on a little stool hammering metal... he looked like a little elf.' The trio quickly acquired a habit of convening at the end of each day's work in the nearby King's Cafe, scoffing deep-friend potato fritters in a bread roll at 80p per cholesterol-packed throw. It was the cheapest item on the menu and, according to Dougie, just the thing after 'a hard day in the art studio sweating... to line your stomach before you'd get twatted on cheap lager.' Serving up said beverage at the Glasgow School of Art bar was Neil, who worked there part-time and befriended Fran on his very first day.

Alcohol was very definitely the Travis members' 'preference', not drugs, as Dougie explains. 'Art schools are full of people who drink. People expect them to be full of these pale, fey boys sitting in the corner, drinking tea, and talking about Keats or something, but they're actually full of booze monsters!' Indeed, Fran recounted how one fellow student died from taking so much acid that 'one day he just never flashed back. The thing is you're institutionalised as a student, none of it's real. And once you leave, you can see how mad it all is.'

Prior to hitting the bar, the crucial timetable of the day started with coffee at nine, a cigarette and coffee break in the middle of the morning, then a meet at the Vic Bar at twelve for a pint and a cheese toastie. What money was left after these between-class repasts would be spent on the aforementioned 'fritters in a bap' before going out on the town. Ports of call might include the Horseshoe Bar, where Neil Primrose worked, King Tut's Wah-Wah Hut ('I used to think I want to get on that poster,') or the Tunnel Club, where Fran had pulled pints on a part-time basis to supplement his grant before band matters took precedence.

For six months in 1992, Fran used the La's 'Feelin'' as the record he'd put on to get him out of bed each morning – and even though it fared much less well than the Liverpool group's more famed (and often revived) 'There She Goes', he felt it taught him a great songwriting lesson - to capture the listener's attention in the first eight bars of a song. His writing, which had begun in 1990 with 'emulating people and generally faffing about', was coming on apace. As Dougie explained a decade later, the subjects Fran chose were universal ones 'and that's why he strikes a chord. Everybody feels love, fear and guilt… he's a very emotional man.'

Fran was, however, finding it hard to carve a niche surrounded by the excessive music coming out of the 1980s and early 1990s. So he returned to the verities of an earlier age, most notably Canadian singer-songwriter Joni Mitchell. By this time, she was hardly a hip name to drop, and indeed would record sparingly during a decade where health problems persuaded her to take time away from the rock 'n' roll treadmill, but for Fran her lyrics were truly inspirational. Her 1971 album *Blue*, with very little more than voice and piano or guitar, was rarely off his record player, while he cites 'The Circle Game' (the closing track from another, earlier album *Ladies Of The Canyon*) as the song he'd like to have played at his funeral.

In the summer of 1993, aged 19, Fran had come to something of a career crossroads. Cycling to the School of Art, he'd padlock his bike to a large piece of sculpture outside that read: 'Do You Enjoy What You Do?' Quite a question for a young man about to leave his teens. Painting was not satisfying his creative urge – he started plenty of character studies, but finished all too few – so the answer to the question had to be a negative.

His sudden departure from the educational scene is something he now describes as 'my biggest failure in life'... even though he insists 'a degree in art is as useful as a man's nipple!' Dougie meanwhile was given a shock when he next visited the library to find that Fran had taken out some books in his name and they'd been found in a skip! Fran puts this down to the fact he left everything behind - his paintings, brushes, bag, overalls and portfolio.

At least Fran could now could channel his creative energies into full-time songwriting, though it was galling to watch all his friends emerge from art school with prestigious pieces of paper. Not that a degree certificate was the passport to a lucrative and creative career... as Dougie, for one, was well aware. He studied the science of fruit machines or 'puggies' in Scots slang, a machine called Count Cash proving particularly rewarding. 'Five pence a shot, £75 jackpot – that's how me and Andy survived some weeks! You've got your bus fare home, now do you risk it? Maybe you'll have to walk home, but maybe you'll have a brilliant night.'

When he couldn't rely on the 'puggies' to make ends meet, he took a bewildering string of shop jobs – camping equipment, high-fashion shoes, jeans – to get by, and it was while selling footwear that he first ran into Neil Primrose. This brings the story back to Glass Onion, the name by which Andy and Neil's band Running Red were now known. Fran saw them play at the Horseshoe Bar - taking their name from a Beatles *White Album* favourite, the female-fronted band had moved away from cabaret to a style of Adult-Oriented-Rock that took musical cues from American behemoths Jefferson Starship. Fran's opinion of their set was 'shit songs but they were really together' – and thus he saw his opening… so into the ranks he came, thanks to his friendship with Neil. At this point, Dougie was yet to join the band, so their numbers were made up by two brothers whose surname was Martyn.

It was an eerily parallel manoeuvre to Noel Gallagher's takeover of Liam's band, named Rain after another Beatles song. But whereas Noel allowed 'our kid' to stay, the girl (whose name no-one now remembers) had to go.

'We were rubbish, like most bands are when they start out. And, like most bands do, you go along and you kinda cut your teeth, playin' toilets everywhere.

'We were rubbish,' Fran agrees. 'Like most bands are when they start out. And, like most bands do, you go along and you kinda cut your teeth, playin' toilets everywhere. But as it progressed, something had to change. In a way, it was like the youngest member of the band turnin' around and sayin', "Right, I'm gonna be the leader now."'

The band played many local venues over the next few months, plus a couple of university balls of which Fran recalls, 'looking at the girls in their lovely dresses, all covered in puke, crying at the end of the night with their knickers round their ankles'. They gathered a cult following, but Fran felt they were going round in circles.

Having decided the songs were crap, Fran took over as main songwriter which instantly gave the set list an added level of consistency. As a statement of his intent, he signed on the dole, took off to Millport, a holiday resort on the west coast of Scotland, and hired a chalet off-season to get his head together 'with the sole intention of writing the best song I'd written.' He came back with 'All I Want To Do Is Rock.'

His musical inspirations were a long way from most late teens/early twenties, and he's admitted he traced a line back from interviews he'd read with Joni Mitchell in which she revealed the artists she rated. She talked of Bob Dylan, which led Fran to Woody Guthrie who raved about The Band which led him to watch *The Last Waltz*, the Martin Scorsese film, which pointed him towards Neil Young and Eric Clapton...

On returning from the chalet, Fran brought a new dynamism with him, and events took a better turn when his mum came forth with the £600 needed to record a demo tape. On the strength of this, Sony Music in London were prepared to offer Fran a publishing deal – but their contact Charlie Pinder had to get his boss, Blair McDonald, to rubber-stamp the agreement. The pair ventured north of the border to see the band play at the Stones Bar in Edinburgh in October 1995.

The evening was by no means a triumph. Two songs in, and with a drunken, unruly audience in the house, the PA system blew up. All the lights went out and a huge fight broke out. Then one guy accused another of chatting up his girlfriend and it kicked off again. The police were called while Fran and his band watched in horror, their dreams of stardom seemingly going up in smoke. Thankfully, the chaos of the night didn't change anyone's minds – the first song had been their greatest track, 'All I Want To Do Is Rock' and the deal was sealed with a handshake. Neither side has had cause to regret it yet...

Emboldened by this stroke of good fortune, the band entered a Scottish talent contest, the prize being a £2000 grant to fly to New York where the influential New Music Seminar was held annually.

Needless to say, they won, but a rule change meant they were never able to attend the Seminar or collect the winnings.

Lady Luck, having kicked them in the crotch, then offered a consolatory kiss in the unlikely shape of Niko Bolas. Despite not being a high profile name, Bolas had actually worked as a studio engineer with a host of big names including Neil Young and the Rolling Stones, as well as having produced one of Fran's all-time favourite albums, the 'Hindu Love Gods' collaboration between REM and singer-songwriter Warren Zevon.

Bolas was in Scotland when he caught a radio session by the band and, liking what he heard, journeyed to meet them. Fran has likened him to big-screen nanny Mary Poppins in imparting good habits and making them 'play properly, like a band.' He also told Fran to 'write what I believe in, and not tell lies.' It was a short relationship, but suffice to say the quartet have always been grateful for what they gained from it. And three years later when they played in New York, Bolas was there to hear the opening song in their set dedicated to him from the stage.

Fran credits the man with giving them their first pointers to studio success. 'We were working with Niko, who had produced Keith Richards, and it was him who taught us about the angels. One day, he was working with Keith, and Keith had done something on the guitar. Niko played the tape back and said, "How the fuck did you do that?" And Keith went, "Ah, it's the angels, mate!" Niko started getting into the philosophy, and he passed it on to us. 'The angels' is like an X-word for maybe nature or something.'

Having shed their Jefferson Starship pretensions, Glass Onion are said by those who remember them to have purveyed guitar pop in an anarchic, Wonder Stuff-type vein. It's also said that Fran Healy wore a surgeon's outfit on stage for the new line-up's first gig, which also found him throwing sweets into the audience taken from a large suitcase. Coincidentally, non-member Dougie introduced the band that night and enjoyed his role as master of ceremonies so much that he had to be dragged off stage. Glass Onion released four demo songs on a privately pressed EP, containing 'Dream On', 'The Day Before', 'Free Soul' and 'Whenever She Comes Around' – highly collectable rarities by now, of course.

Whatever disparaging remarks Fran may have said about the group since – 'we were shit, but I always thought we'd prevail' – schoolfriend Robert Elliott reckons they were hot stuff live. 'They were a brilliant band and we all said at the time that they would make it big. It was weird as hell, because we used to sit and jam together along with another friend and dream about one day headlining at the Barrowlands, and he's actually done it! And all those girls screaming at him... lucky bastard!'

Initially, Fran was so paranoid about his guitar-playing abilities that he used to go on stage with a guitar with no strings, strumming away to build up his confidence. Then, one night whilst playing a gig at a club called Nice N'Sleazy, there was a power failure. As the crowd began to get restless, Fran plucked up the courage to sing an unplugged version of 'She's So Strange', which was met with rapturous applause.

This was certainly an improvement on a less impressive gig at a place called the Clyde Bar in Helensborough, Scotland, in 1994 where, in a somewhat inebriated state, Fran lost his guitar lead and was standing on stage looking for it. After five minutes of confused searching, the sound engineer walked from his desk, through the crowd, on to the stage, and took the lead off the mike stand right from under Fran's nose! He turned to Fran and said "Come on mate, get a grip."

Travis had become Travis not long after Fran's take-over bid, assuming the name of the drifter character played by Harry Dean Stanton in Wim Wenders' cult film *Paris, Texas*. But there was still a hangover from Glass Onion in the shape of the Martyn brothers on keyboards and bass.

They would unfortunately play the Pete Best role as the member(s) who left just before fame and fortune struck. While Fran admits he felt 'massive guilt' at their departure in March 1996, the death of his beloved grandfather at around about the same time claimed any spare feelings he might have had hanging round.

Besides, it sounds as if there was a musical mis-match going on; Neil has described the bass-playing brother as modelling himself on jazz-rock virtuoso Mark King of Level 42 fame. Keyboards no longer played a part in the future of the band; Fran was now a Telecaster-toting frontman par excellence, meshing more than adequately with Andy's lead lines. Travis would be a quartet from this moment forth... but who would fill the fourth musician role?

The finger soon pointed at Dougie Payne, who'd by now graduated from Glasgow School of Art with a first class degree in sculpture but remained grossly under-employed. He fitted snugly as a personality... the only problem was he couldn't play the bass! 'That didn't bother me,' he later told *Q* magazine, 'but the thought of joining a band I'd known for two years did.'

It seems there were also outside influences at work in the shape of Sony Music. The publisher wanted a new bass player and for the band to relocate to London. Fran told them he had a new bassist (he didn't) but immediately had the brainwave of asking Dougie. 'So I borrowed Neil's girlfriend's old bass, went straight around to Dougie's house, put it on him, and stood him in front of the mirror. I said, "Woof! You were born to play the bass." He still said no, but I got him in the end.'

Dougie spent two weeks playing along to a cassette, with sporadic visits from Fran to check on his progress, and before long he was a fully fledged member. As the last person to join Travis, Dougie had to fit in with the prevailing musical directions. His first task was to familiarise himself with the loping Levon Helm shuffle beloved of Neil and exemplified by 'Up On Cripple Creek' from 1970's classic, sepia-toned *The Band* – not exactly standard listening for someone of his age! This was the first American music he'd ever

liked, guilty as he was of being into white British bands. However, 'this immediately struck every chord for me.'

Dougie's family were surprised their son went into music full time - they knew he enjoyed it but never felt he would class it as anything more than a hobby. That said, Dougie was working at the Levi's store in town when Fran asked him to join the band, which perhaps reflected how much financial potential lay in his art career. Besides, he viewed the basic principles of both mediums as the same - communication.

'We just went and hid away for a year. It paid off... we got good.'

The new quartet made their debut in a spare room over the Horseshoe bar, where Neil still worked part-time. All are now agreed it was a near-spiritual experience, where 'the stars had come into line and fireworks went off.' Fran, ever the movie buff, likened it to the scene in *The Wizard Of Oz* where the main characters set off down the Yellow Brick Road... although in Travis's case the road led to a local Indian restaurant where they gorged themselves, content they now had the line-up they'd been seeking. Indeed, Andy, convinced things were on the turn, put his extra-curricular moneymaking activities – running a mobile disco for the over-60s and working weekends as marshal on a paintball site – on indefinite hold.

The room two floors above the Horseshoe would henceforth be the scene of ever more frantic activity, as Travis sharpened up their act. It was an all-day experience that took its cue from Fran's creative input - he'd write alone from midday to six with a four-track, after which the rest of the band came in to rehearse until 11pm. The band had offered to pay pub manager Dave for the electricity, but he refused to take anything.

Eventually, however, they turned their back on this localised rehearse-record-rehearse policy. Their continued failure to find a record deal, despite a year's worth of rehearsals only (and no gigs), frustrated them sufficiently that they cut adrift from the circle of people working with the band at that time. 'We just went and hid away for a year. It paid off... we got good.'

'The sound was terrible, the audience couldn't give a shit but we were up there having a ball.'

The first new song the four-piece band tackled and made their own was 'All I Want To Do Is Rock', whose anthemic qualities would prove talismanic. Then came a one-off gig where they proved to the punters what they already knew. It was the first of March 1996. 'The sound was terrible, the audience couldn't give a shit but we were up there having a ball. I'd look to my left and there was a best mate on guitar, to my right a best mate on bass, behind me a best mate on drums. We were grinning madly, we just knew. Something clicked. It's been legendary ever since.'

Within weeks, Fran and Dougie had hatched a plan to take Travis to the epicentre of the music world - London. The move wasn't something anyone would take lightly. Neil had broken off his engagement as well as his job at the Horseshoe. All were agreed they'd give it six months and see how it went. The farewell to Glasgow started with an 'utterly shambolic,' gig in the School of Art's Vic Bar. Now, more than ever, Fran knew he was right to pursue music over élitist art: 'I despise the notion that ordinary folk don't understand.' He continued, 'at a certain point, I decided that if I ever did anything artistic again, it had to be accessible to a majority of people. And what art form is more suited than music?'

CHAPTER FOUR

LONDON CALLING

What are the odds they'll put a blue plaque on 19, Chesterfield Gardens, London, N4 someday? That semi-detached residence with its weed-strewn garden in the suburb of Haringey was to be the nerve centre for Travis's campaign of world domination. Dougie remembers their communal life there to that enjoyed by the Monkees – that zany American made-for-television pop group of the 1960s so beloved of himself and Andy. Their first summer in London was a glorious one which they all remember with great affection: look at the back cover of *Good Feeling* for confirmation. 'Our landlord looked exactly like (Nintendo computer game character) Super Mario... we always thought he was burying people.'

For the band, moving in together had been a new experience even though they knew each other well, since all bar Neil had lived with their mums when students. Now lodging together, on the dole and living in student quality digs, they lived a life very similar to their previous art school existence: 'You can't afford to go out on 35 quid a week, so you just stay in the whole time.'

Andy insists the conditions at Chesterfield Gardens were considerably more sanitary that you'd have supposed, claiming 'the bathroom was practically sacred.' The atmosphere in the house was harmonious, and even when tension mounted, the friends were astute enough to go for a beer or a walk until things simmered down. This mutually respectful attitude was perhaps a precursor of their latter-day gang mentality for which Travis have become so renowned.

London had got quite used to invading Celts in years past. Once upon a time the image of the Tartan Army heading for the Capital was enough to have strong men quaking and mothers locking up their daughters – who can forget the image of the Wembley crossbar being violently snapped? Ironically Travis's decision to relocate, lock stock and barrel, to the big city coincided with the first football meeting of England and Scotland since 1989 – and the first at Wembley since a year before that. The European Championship draw had pitched the Auld Enemy against each other... but sadly for the lads, the English would maintain their five-game unbeaten streak and take the honours 2-0.

So if Scotsmen in London weren't exactly thin on the ground in June 1996, then Travis could at least explore their new surroundings under cover of anonymity. That wouldn't last for long, though. Fortunately, any chance of what Fran called 'the six-month plan' going wrong and them having to 'slink home with our tail between our legs' was soon to be dispelled. They signed to Wildlife Management, an outfit which guided the careers of acts like Brand New Heavies, Tim Simenon (of Bomb the Bass fame) and had helped singer-songwriter Tasmin 'Sleeping Satellites' Archer to No. 1. It seemed an unlikely matching – after all, none of those acts, however meritorious, could be described as a rock band – but a meeting in the World's End pub in Camden between Fran, Dougie and Ian McAndrew set the seal on an arrangement that continues successfully today.

Soon afterwards, the still-unsigned Travis performed their first show at the Dublin Castle in Camden, in front of an audience estimated conservatively at around 25. This lack of a record deal would soon change, but not before commencing an ongoing tour schedule starting at the Army & Navy pub in Chelmsford.

For anyone unaware of London geography, Camden Town is a hub of aspiring guitar bands. Aside from long-established venues like Dingwall's Dancehall, a late-night club venue, the Electric Ballroom (host to many legendary punk-era gigs) and the relatively new Jazz Café, there are a number of pubs where the crowd can be guaranteed to include a high percentage of record company talent scouts.

'There's a beautiful moment when you write a great song, another when the red light in the studio goes on and you record it, and the third is playing a gig.'

But there was still much work to be done on the music, and Travis came to regard the rehearsal studio as their second home. They'd daily hone their craft in what would add up to 40-hour weeks; hard work by anyone's yardstick. It was certainly a step up, environment-wise, from the room above the Horseshoe – a fact underlined by the flight cases sitting around stencilled with household names like Suede and Pulp. Andy once saw Jarvis arrive, Mary-Poppins-like - on a push-bike!

The music was coming together well, but manager McAndrew

was having a problem with the name. They'd ditched Travis for... Red Telephone Box, a moniker you can hardly imagine gracing the world's foremost fly-poster sites. On enquiring as to their previous handle, McAndrew demanded they change it back immediately – and being affable, reasonable chaps, they agreed. Fran had initially been inspired by the multitude of red phone boxes in London - in northern climes they had been out of service for some time, appearing only as showers or greenhouses. 'We decided to go back to Travis, (but) we thought Red Telephone Box's still quite a good name to call the record label.'

You're not a real band, of course, in the eyes of the world until you release a record. Putting one of his songs on the market had indeed been the culmination of a long-cherished dream, though everything for Fran Healy has its context. 'Writing, recording and playing live all have their own special moments. There's a beautiful moment when you write a great song, another when the red light in the studio goes on and you record it, and the third is playing a gig, working your arse off and knowing you've got through to the audience. The satisfaction is that people are getting it.'

Realistically, Travis's first release wasn't going to change the world as we know it overnight... especially as only 750 copies were going to be pressed. To underline Travis's 'credibility', these were going to be in ten-inch vinyl format on the Red Telephone Box label, completing that neat compromise over the band's name. And so it was that 'All I Want To Do Is Rock' hit the streets as a strictly limited edition fashion in October 1996.

The song was a mid-paced wall-of-sound guitar anthem bemoaning the fact that the object of the singer's affection doesn't do anything but work. Its author compares it with the Beatles 'Help', an observation that's not as far-fetched as it seems. Both songs share a certain urgency, and both start very directly on the letter H: 'hey' and 'help.'

Melody Maker reckoned 'All I Want To Do Is Rock' deserved to be their 'Single of the Week. 'Your first anything – first drink, first shag – is always the best,' Fran later reminisced, and that's why it's special.' At the time they were in New York being taken round record companies by their management (they'd sign with Epic, a subsidiary of Sony), and just as they checked into their hotel, the desk clerk pulled out a fax of the cutting. News was travelling fast...

The next name to loom large in the Travis story was Andy Macdonald, a young music-business entrepreneur whose Go! Discs operation (Paul Weller, Portishead, Beautiful South, etc) had recently been consumed by the PolyGram multi-national. He was looking to start a new venture as soon as legal niceties allowed, and was on the hunt for suitable acts to sign. A Travis demo tape had found its way to him, and what he heard led to an assignation with Fran at a pub in London's seedy King's Cross where indie hopefuls A Secret Goldfish were playing. Fran laughingly recounted their encounter thus: 'He shuffles in, sidles up to the bar and goes, "You're Fran, aren't you?" I thought, "Oh man, I've been in London a month and my mother warned me about people like him!"'

Macdonald had been intrigued by the demo's two songs – 'All I Want To Do Is Rock' and 'Funny Thing'. The mixture of a full-on feedback anthem and an emotion-drenched ballad provided an unusual dichotomy. 'I just wondered what was in-between.' He found out when he caught a show at the Dublin Castle, impressed by the songs, Fran's voice and the band's general mix of humour and passion. This was the band that his new record label would be built upon, though progress was inevitably slow at first, not least because he hadn't left Go! Discs when he first saw them.

'We decided we could stay in Glasgow and do nothing, or we could go to where the music business is and become pop stars.'

For their part, the band were taken aback by Macdonald's honesty and artistic understanding and were very keen to work with him immediately. In Dougie's opinion, he couldn't have found a better act on which to build his hopes: 'We're very dependable too – we get the work done and we won't let the side down.'

A connection was made and a deal eventually done, a rumoured £100,000 advance cheque being written on Macdonald's own personal account. Intriguingly, despite Go! Discs' star-studded roster, the group that kicked off the label, a Sheffield trio called the Box, would never be heard of again. Would that be the fate of Travis and this new label, to be called Independiente?

Whatever the future held, Fran felt his decision to move operations down south had already been more than justified. 'We decided we could stay in Glasgow and do nothing, or we could go to where the music business is and become pop stars, so we decided to burn our bridges.' Despite being told their move was a risk, the band felt confident enough that they would eventually succeed.

The anonymity with which Travis's four members had previously enjoyed was astonishingly to be threatened in November with their first television appearance – no local cable station, either, but the national BBC2 channel. Every band dreams of *Top Of The Pops* but every credible band rates *Later With Jools Holland* as an equally important career milestone. What's more, you can sneak onto the *Later* line-up even if you haven't had a hit yet, because the programme's policy is very much that of selection on merit.

Just as when the Sex Pistols appeared on television and swore at presenter Bill Grundy, there are many thousands of people who now make out they were tuned in when Travis took their televisual bow on 25 November, alongside such acts as Sting, Tricky and Motown balladmeister Lionel Richie, whose million-selling ballad 'Easy' was probably the kitsch highlight of the transmission. The connection with the soul superstar was particularly interesting for Fran, who recalls buying 'Hello' back in the 1980s for his Grandad.

Travis, of course, had watched the programme before and all admitted to having some serious stage fright when first placed in front of the cameras. 'We were on the other side of the studio when Jools introduced us,' he explains, 'and then suddenly the camera came flying past him, straight towards me… I was like, "Wow!"' Fortunately, their rendition of 'All I Want To Do Is Rock' was quite simply breath-taking.

Amazingly, when Travis met Lionel Richie afterwards, he told them how much he had been impressed by their performance - wonder what he'd have said had he realised that, as he rehearsed 'Easy,' Dougie and Andy were singing the backing vocals to each other!

With an assured TV debut under their belts, Travis's next appointment was with the recording studio and sessions for what would become their first album, *Good Feeling*. These took the band well away from their adopted home city – purely for the reason that everywhere their producer Steve Lillywhite wanted to use was booked solid! Lillywhite was nothing short of a legendary name, having worked with acts as diverse as Peter Gabriel, Joan Armatrading and U2. He'd also put in time with Scots legends like Simple Minds and Big Country, so had first-hand knowledge of the Celtic psyche. Certainly, a name like his was rare indeed on debut albums of bands signed to independent labels...

Due to the lack of recording space in London, the decision was made to cross the Atlantic and record in the States. Better still, the chosen venue was Bearsville Studios in Woodstock, New York State – a venue known not only for being the site of the world's most famous rock festival but the habitat of Bob Dylan and his group, The Band. The vibe in the studio, a small quiet building surrounded by snow-covered trees, was 'fantastic.'

On the wall of the studio was a photo called 'The Founding Fathers', a mixture of the studios original owners along with other famous musicians. So the band set up a team photo of their own in the same format as the original, with engineers, studio bosses and even the cook as a memento of their time in the Catskills.

It was indeed an environment everyone involved found both relaxing and stimulation. The isolated location meant distractions were few and far between, allowing the band to focus on the job in hand. And this was a band which knew exactly where it was going - the whole album took just *four* days to commit to tape.

Fortunately, and despite his status as a studio superstar, Steve

Lillywhite fell in with their wishes rather than trying to impose his own. While he might have been expected to favour modern studio techniques, he agreed to let Travis record each song as a band rather than separately layering the instruments one on top of the other. Mistakes were corrected as and when they were spotted. Though Fran was surprised at the speed in which it all came together, he was delighted: 'We would record a song, play it twice and Steve would just say, "Yeah, that's it, next one." We were like, 'Whaaat?!'

The result was a record that many people felt sounded more American than British. Not surprising perhaps, given that REM and the late Jeff Buckley had also recorded there in recent times. That was a big enough thrill for Dougie, who rates Jeff's gig at the Glasgow School of Art 'the best I've ever seen. Just him, his electric guitar, and a pint of Guinness. Astonishing, totally magic.' But for Fran, the Bearsville bonus was that Travis did not sound like yet another Brit-pop band, detached as they were from their native musical environment.

'It was pissing with rain. Everywhere I go.'

During their two week tenancy, the band stayed in a real-life haunted house in a place called Purple Creek. Fran for one was totally convinced: 'I was in the house by myself a couple of times and things started going mental. At one point, I was just leaving the house and someone whistled at me from the room I was leaving. I looked around and there was obviously no one there. It was a big old strong whistle. It was fucking weird. Pretty scary.'

The only disappointment of the fortnight was Fran's discovery that the Woodstock Festival of 1969 never actually happened in or even near the town that bestowed the event's name, but in fact

25 miles down the road, after the license was revoked at the last minute.

They weren't to know it as they emerged from the studio, but Travis would have to wait eight long months for the fruits of their labours to be made available to the public. Andy Macdonald was not in any hurry - happily, the boys were content to go along with his masterplan, largely because they believed in his vision of running a record company honourably and with sympathy for the artist.'

With no imminent release of the album on the cards, Fran decided to take a post-recording holiday, hoping to catch some sun (Lillywhite said he was too white), but his week in Israel saw continual torrential rain. 'It was pissing with rain. Everywhere I go.' Of course there'd be a song in it...

Christmas 1996 came and went, as did gigs with Embrace and Ultrasound, and, by July 1997, when they journeyed to New York to do press Travis were primed for stardom... even though their reception in the hotel where Independiente had booked them was far from welcoming. Thrown out of the restaurant for lighting up their duty free Silk Cuts, ejected from the lobby for drinking mineral water straight out the bottle, refused booze in the restaurant because 'that's where we serve food; the bar serves alcohol', they were still chipper enough to pose with one of the city's trademark yellow and black cabs. One can only assume the driver had been enticed elsewhere with food, booze or, indeed, duty-fee Silk Cuts - while his pals lounged over the bonnet or holding a door, Fran insisted on standing atop the roof and imitating a Scotland goal celebration!

Dougie immediately fell in love with the Big Apple, a connection which was later reinforced by an American girlfriend. Fran was really enjoying the ever-changing backdrop: 'It's like fuel for us. We moved from Glasgow to London for that very reason. We've all been given legs, we were meant to use them.' With the long-awaited release of *Good Feeling*, the band would be putting their legs, luggage and passports to extensive use in the weeks and months ahead...

CHAPTER FIVE

FEELING ALRIGHT

The band's second single was, in many ways, as important as their first, for three reasons. It was kicking off their career on a brand new record label, it was the first Travis release to be available to more than just a favoured few and it was the record that would either confirm them as one of 1997's brightest hopes or consign them to the dumper. There had been many a review, both of their recorded and live output, citing Travis as the next Radiohead, so in many ways an intimidating precedent had been set.

Fran was prepared to live with such labels, for the moment anyway, rightly acknowledging that they are there to provide listeners of the approximate sound of a new band. Besides, he pointed out that this was only one part of the picture. 'Radiohead are fantastic, but they're a bit of a "monkey band." They only have one emotion or method of expression. There is something limited in that approach that doesn't deal with all sides of things. For us, it's as important to lift people up as it is to bring them down.'

Travis were certainly out to prove that point by coming up with something completely unexpected for their new single – a glam anthem Suede would have been proud of with lyrics guaranteed to send *Daily Mail* readers scurrying to their typewriters with gritted teeth and knotted brow - namely 'U16 Girls'. On the face of it, it seemed that *Select*'s appraisal of the lyrics as 'based on some unsavoury personal trawl through a twilight of underage sex' was accurate. However, the song was actually a very direct warning from the band to those of a paedophilic persuasion to restrict their activities. With yobbo backing vocals (contributed, tongue-in-cheek album credits would later claim, to the 'Joyous Lake Singers'), this was certainly not subtle stuff. Whatever, it was a release guaranteed to get a reaction. Love or hate.

'An upbeat blast of pop-rock whipped on by a great voice that somehow combined Marti Pellow and Kurt Cobain.'

Reviewers certainly got in a twist as they lined up in opposing factions. They were called the 'new Longpigs,' and 'a 90s Glitter Band,' amongst other things. One reviewer said 'Why do I hate this band so much?' *New Musical Express* homed in on 'a pervasive sense of dumbness that surrounds it. Like the Ramones or the Cult, Travis reduce rock 'n' roll to an utterly simplistic world of girls and alcohol.' Fortunately, there was good press too - *Q* called 'U16 Girls' 'an upbeat blast of pop-rock whipped on by a great voice that somehow combined Marti Pellow and Kurt Cobain.'

The single also introduced Travis to national radio for the first time. Fran was called by a friend who told him they were on but, by the time he tuned in, all he caught was the last few chords. Dougie and Neil had better luck, hearing their record on air while patronising a local off-licence. 'We just walked in to buy some beers,' explains Dougie, 'and there it was. Our song. Coming out of the radio. We thought the guy had his radio tuned in to some indie station, and we said, "What's that?" and he said, "Radio 1!" We started jumping up and down and got him to turn it up and started air-guitaring in the middle of the shop. No shame.' After Doug and Andy had finished their dance, the owner came up with a far-fetched but ultimately impressive prediction: 'You guys are gonna be the next millionaires!'

'We just walked in to buy some beers and there it was. Our song. Coming out of the radio.'

Fran has been asked a million and one times if 'U16 Girls' is based upon personal experience. 'The answer to that,' says Fran, 'is no. It's not based upon experience... It's a fictitious song. The woman who I met in Paris in the second verse wasn't under 16; she was actually 36. She was Japanese, and I met her in Paris when I was 17, and we walked around Paris all day going to all the exhibitions together.' He used the title, he explains, 'cos I thought it sounded like an old World War II bomber.'

The B-side of the single, 'Hazy Shade Of Gold', started a trend of tracks not being included on albums that fans could only get by buying the single. *Select* described it as 'a twisted Faces-style rocker besmirched by the sound of an out-of-tune pub piano and Franny soundly castigating the other band members for the poor quality of their apparently sauce-wrecked playing.'

This song didn't make the debut album – unlike 'U16 Girls', which appeared as Track 2 behind, suitably enough, its predecessor. And God knows what the critics would've said if they'd known the original title of 'All I Want to Do Is Rock' had been 'All I Want To Do Is Fuck... ' Actually, that was a bit of whimsy in a press pack prepared by the record company for journalists that ultimately ended up backfiring. The band vowed never to try to be ironic or overly-clever in press releases again. The song was actually about the crystalisation of Fran's mind and motivation at the time they moved to London. This reflected Fran's emotional, rather than cerebral approach to songwriting: 'Whatever you write about, if it comes from your heart then people will get it. If you just write from your mind, then you must be a brilliant actor.'

The rest of the first album, *Good Feeling*, was a modest success. If record-buyers were already familiar with Tracks 1 and 2, then Track 3, 'The Line Is Fine', was guaranteed to snag the attention straight away. It began with a self-deprecating opening line before chugging along for four minutes in slightly less memorable fashion. Like all the songs on *Good Feeling* it came from Fran's pen, and he took the vocal honours here with only Andy's increasingly atonal guitar to distract the listener. Rasping on the playout in time-honoured John Lennon/Liam Gallagher fashion couldn't disguise the fact that this song was not going to take the listener to another level... a lot of sound and fury, signifying little. Like many of the lesser songs here, though, it was a perfectly passable stage number.

Much more promising was Track 4, 'A Good Day To Die' which might just have taken its cue from the previous song's imagery of standing on a window ledge. Alternatively, there might have been a *Star Trek* fan in the house: Lieutenant Worf, the resident Klingon on the USS *Enterprise*, was apt to greet news of impossible opposing odds with the epithet: 'Today is a good day to die'.

As Fran revealed, though, there was a less space-age origin to the phrase, claiming it drew on Red Indian culture's view that this was the best day of your life.' Whatever its origins, it was a decided improvement on the working title, 'Handful of Pies'...

The imagery of brick walls, footballs and broken windows somehow seemed to bespeak the band's Glasgow home – but quite why death was on Fran's mind wasn't really explained. One critic could see this as similar to the Verve by acknowledging 'the sunshine that slashes the darkest of clouds.' Interestingly, that band's *Urban Hymns* dominated the radio scene at this time, depriving albums like *Good Feeling* of much of the oxygen of airplay.

'There's so much stuff about, but take away all the shite and there'd only be about 20 bands worth listening to.'

Next came the title track, with its offbeat keyboards adding an almost reggae-like feeling to Neil's shuffling drums. Again though, it's a wordless vocal hook that provides the chorus not the title phrase which crops up in the first line and again in sundry places about the lyric. Like so many of the songs here, 'Good Feeling' was inspired by a long-time girlfriend three years Fran's junior who he'd go to see on the 44 bus every day for two and a half years – he lived at one end of the route, she at the other. Her family were unhappy at his lack of a job with prospects, and 'Good Feeling', written after she'd ended the relationship, was supposed to convey the message that music was the biggest thing in his life.

Expressing grief as well as justification, the middle eight of this song seems very noisy and the volume continues to the end of the song, which carries a piano solo somehow reminiscent of 1980s ska-meisters Madness. Then we get a reprise of the first verse by Fran and piano alone to end on a relatively peaceful note.

A burst of feedback wakes everything up for 'Midsummer Night's Dreaming' – a Beatlesque burst of pop energy that inevitably conjures up early Oasis, especially the boozing and puking reference. The first real stroke of songwriting genius for some time comes with 'Tied To The '90s', a Kinks-meets-Small Faces-style romp through some fairly simplistic lyrics. The 1980s were worse than the 1990s, but that's not saying much, which is why the chorus alternated between being tired of the 90s and tied to the 1990s. 'That's what annoys and intrigues me about the decade,' said Fran, continuing 'there's so much stuff about, but take away all the shite and there'd only be about 20 bands worth listening to.' At any event, this was an anthem, and one lauded by a critic as 'a traditional rock 'n' roll song that marries a comprehensive knowledge of the past to an altogether more intangible vision of the future.'

A welcome change of pace comes with 'I Love You Anyways', an acoustic ballad laced with reverbed lead guitar from Andy that tells of Fran's Glasgow youth with its references to the cinema, art galleries, city walls and buses. This was a real pointer to the next album and much more effective for the understatement. The hissy exhalation of breath on some of the words only adds to the reality of the delivery… and when you hear that the subtitle, 'for CF', refers to the girlfriend he loved for two and a half years before losing, you realise just how real it is.

It would have been a challenging song to attempt to hold the attention within a noisy public bar, and therein lay the main Achilles heel of *Good Feeling*. By banging down their live set in almost its entirety, Travis had come up with something that would sound better delivered from the stage than via the sterile medium of the compact disc. This song more than any so far, with its 'Abbey Road'-style arpeggios from Andy 'George Harrison' Dunlop, was stunning in its understatement, and you'd look twice at the CD timer which would tell you that it clocked in at five and a half minutes. It certainly didn't outstay its welcome.

Back to the unrelenting percussion and bang-bang rhythm guitar

for Track 9, 'Happy'. Having been entranced by the 'arch pop classicism' of 'All I Want To Do Is Rock', *Guitar* magazine's reviewer thought this was 'naive Bay City Roller stuff'; some critics suggested it was a track about smoking dope but Fran has never substantiated this.

Then, though, we meet the second gem of the album: 'More Than Us', a song so delicate the Art of Noise's Anne Dudley was brought in to add the orchestration. Again, it was a song you couldn't hear them belting out at the Dublin Castle, but another clear pointer to the sound and style that would soon make Travis a household name.

''Funny Thing' does sound like Radiohead. I have to agree with you... but there are worse things to sound like.'

Almost as if Travis had got hold of the right end of the stick three days into the session, 'Falling Down' continued the downbeat mood and was rewarded by a lyrical guitar solo which boosted Fran to one of his most impassioned vocals.

A spooky occurrence occurred on 'Falling Down', as Fran explained. 'It ended up with this great tambourine on in the middle, even though we never recorded any tambourine on it. Then we realised that a tambourine had been lying on one of the speakers and that had started it vibrating. Of course, Neil, our drummer, was pissed off: "Aw, fuck, man, that should have been me doing that".' One of Keith Richards' aforementioned 'accidents' perhaps...?

Last but far from least comes 'Funny Thing', a song that starts with Fran's solo voice and guitar, its Abba-like verse-melody then veering off on a course of its own. The lyrical conclusion ends a schizophrenic album in downbeat mood. The building intensity and Fran's keening vocal were clearly going to invite continued comparisons with Radiohead, something he cheerfully admitted to one intrepid questioner. "Funny Thing' does sound like Radiohead. I have to agree with you... but there are worse things to sound like.'

'The cutest, Scottishest indie band in the world!'

The common denominator, he explained, was that most of the songs dealt with relationships. 'There are relationships in everything – the sciences, maths, humans, animals, everywhere... To me, Travis is a room with all the doors open and you can come in and go out whenever you want.'

So if *Good Feeling* found Travis discovering how to sound like themselves and coming up with two different answers, the result wasn't by any means unpleasant. Danny Eccleston of *Q* magazine regarded 'the rattling, effervescent, rockin', sobbin' *Good Feeling* as 'miraculously perfect, as if geneticists had grafted Thom Yorke and Noel Gallagher onto (John Lennon's) Plastic Ono Band and saw that it was good.'

Good Feeling received a generally favourable reception at the hands of other critics too. The press plaudits came from far and wide. At the bottom end of the age scale, *Just Seventeen* reckoned Travis were 'the cutest, Scottishest indie band in the world!', while *The Independent* got rather more verbose: 'With the cocksure front of waltzer fare collectors, they trounce our senses with a bumper box of sonic fireworks.'

New Musical Express's Stuart Bailie was even more complimentary,

praising 'a top party record (with a) rowdy aspect that boogies along with a saving hint of irony. *Good Feeling* contains 12 songs of sturdy brilliance and intermittent beauty... an explosively accomplished exercise in the art of writing thrilling and memorable pop songs.'

Despite the speedy album sessions, one reviewer suggested the record had been 'over-produced', a comment which made Travis laugh. They were proud of their economy of time: 'Atlantic Records used to close the office at the end of the day and then record an album during the night. The next day, they would open up the office again and work on selling the record! I was really pleased that we did the album in four days.'

There wasn't much of a battle plan when it came to promoting the album: after all, Independiente was in its infancy and, as marketing director Tony Crean later admitted, 'it was just let's put out a record, let's get the band on tour... single, single, album.' One stroke of genius, though, was to include reply-paid cards in the album packaging to encourage fans to make themselves known, and the 20,000-strong database they ended up with would prove invaluable in the months to come. For his part, Fran was so taken by having a record in the shops that he actually purchased a copy for himself! Musically, he remained proud of their first long player offering, calling it quite simply 'a collection of cool songs.'

Andy Dunlop came out with something rather more profound. When it was put to him that the band's serious musical persona and off-stage 'gang humour' didn't quite seem to gel, he suggested 'With us, you'll only get the whole story at the end of our career. How many albums that'll be I don't know. But we're not out for the short term.'

Since 'All I Want To Do Is Rock' hadn't reached an audience of more than three figures first time out, Independiente decided to re-issue it in June 1997. But not the original demo that had emerged on the 10-inch. This was a Woodstock re-recording that, in the *New Musical Express's* unbeatable words was 'a re-recorded, altogether dirtier version, more feisty, energised, and covered in feedback muck... it still had Thom Yorke's star-gazing eyes, but it had grown the teeth of a rabid Alsatian and the tonsils of Heavy Stereo having their toenails ripped out.' Phew...

Instead of the original B-sides, 'The Line Is Fine' and 'Funny Thing', both of which had surfaced on the album, they substituted 'Blue On A Black Weekend and 'Combing My Hair' for CD1 and two age-related songs, '20' and '1922', on CD2. The last-named combined the age of Fran and his then-girlfriend, but it was '20' that would become the first of what would become a growing list of hard-to-find favourites. 'It's about sitting in your English class when you're 13, staring at the ceiling, and thinking about how crap it is. Then it goes to 14 and fancying a girl at school, then to 15 when your parents are shouting at you... nothing that should get binned ever gets used as B-sides with us. It's just a really nice song.'

Despite their higher profile, the newly re-issued single only improved one place on 'U16 Girls' chart showing, and a mere two months later was followed by a new song to promote the album. 'Tied To The 90s' would justify that decision, keeping the momentum going and rising as high as the dizzy heights of No. 30. No fewer than three tracks – 'City In The Rain', 'Whenever She Comes Around' and 'Standing On My Own' – accompanied it on the first compact disc, with 'Me Beside You' the tempter on CD2.

Fran was already keen to throw off the 'indie' tag. Travis was making music to be heard by as many people as possible, preferably millions. Besides, after the onslaught of Britpop, 'indie' no longer really existed, with quality British alternative music being a regular feature of all the chart listings. 'But even if it did, there's no great thing about being a hero among 1,000 people worldwide.'

Fran would have his wish... but he'd have to wait a while longer to make all his dreams come true. Had *Good Feeling* sold in larger quantities, Fran later reflected, 'We'd all be living in castles now... It's to do with luck and the time that it comes out. I'm beginning to realise that luck is the most important thing.'

CHAPTER SIX

EVERYBODY ON THE BUS!

One of Travis's first PR jobs to promote the album was scheduled to be a photo shoot for the benefit of *Q* magazine. The gimmick was to be a balloon trip, but for various reasons soon to be detailed, the late-October day ended up as anything other than an up, up and away experience... Fortunately for anyone like Travis's guitarist with an aversion to flight, the Super Sky Trips' balloon situated in a Battersea park didn't actually do any flying beyond its tethering rope.

Unfortunately for everyone bar Andy Dunlop, it was the weather that turned out to be particularly ropy, so plan B was put into operation. Fortunately it didn't involve Battersea's famous Dogs' Home, but a local zoo, where the band gamely attempted to improvise a pastiche of the Beach Boys' *Pet Sounds* album cover of 1966. Said cover was, unfortunately, one of the tamest in rock history, totally unlike the shimmering music contained on the vinyl within.

Maybe the Dogs' Home would have been a better bet, since all suitable non-carnivorous animals – kangaroo, llama, capybara and the rest – had taken shelter from the wind and rain. Also, the *Q* photographer's portable backdrop proved about as sturdy as a windbreak on a storm-tossed beach. It was indeed, as Fran eloquently expressed it, 'a bummer'. To cap it all, as they struck yet another pose, a passing rollerblader fell over on the tarmac, fracturing her ankle. Fran gallantly led the posse running to her aid, and ten minutes or so after he'd whipped out his mobile phone the park was swarming with paramedics, on-lookers, police and several dogs.

'There's only a few things to do in a band, one's recording, one's writing and when you're not doing those two you may as well stay on the road.'

In an effort to get things over with as quickly as possible, a brown mongrel was co-opted to finish the shoot. Clutched firmly by a smiling Fran and a grim-faced Dougie (who'd clearly had enough), its splayed-leg pose ensured the pic was the dog's bollocks in at least one respect.

By the middle of 1997, Travis had played just about every small to middling rock 'n' roll venue Britain had to offer. The list of acts they'd opened for was impressive: Mansun, the Longpigs, Cast, Reef, Dodgy and Paul Weller. 'There's only a few things to do in a band,' said Fran, 'one's recording, one's writing and when you're not doing

CUDDLE
A SNOOZE
TENNIS

GILBE
AND
GEOR
EXHIBITIO

those two you may as well stay on the road.'

Dougie pointed to the efficacy of gaining a grass-roots following through gigging by pointing to the fact that 'All I Want To Do Is Rock' had charted despite radio turning its back on it. His view was that only by seeing a band live could fans be convinced of their worth; conversely, he insisted that the definition of 'a good band' was one that was still good in twenty years time.

It was suitable that, as their first album had finally rolled off the presses and they prepared to hit the road once again, that Travis should take delivery of a new tour bus. Actually, the mere words 'tour bus' hardly did justice to the ten-berth Len Wright Sleeper Coach they inherited. Little wonder the group described it as 'nicer than some of the houses we've lived in.' A fridge, microwave, toilet, video player, Playstation and tartan cushions were among the creature comforts on offer. And since the back wheels had fallen off the band's last vehicle in an impressively scary shower of sparks, it was to be hoped this would last them through to at least the third album, if not beyond. As for in-flight entertainment, half-empty bottles of Tequila and an ever-present pall of cigarette smoke said it all...

Good Feeling entered the UK listings at No. 9 on 20 September 1997, four weeks into the chart reign of Oasis's 1.5 million-selling *Be Here Now*. Radiohead's truly epic *OK Computer* was still in the Top 3 some three months after release, while other close competitors included Genesis, Roni Size's Mercury Music Prize-winning drum and bass act and that year's favourite firestarters, the Prodigy.

The following week would bring an alarming sales slump for *Good Feeling*, which couldn't be put down to a new No. 1 from Ocean Colour Scene. Travis duly slouched down to No. 26 and would spend just one more week in the Top 75, at 53, before slipping out of the reckoning altogether. This, though, was the first stage of the pre-Christmas madness that would see up to five new entries in the Top 10 each week, hits collections from past legends like John Lennon, Queen and David Bowie and, eventually and inevitably, a Spice Girls album. It took the Spices to knock the Verve's all-conquering *Urban Hymns* off the top, so whichever way you look at it, Travis could not have chosen a more testing time to deliver their debut. As far as Travis's boss Andy Macdonald was concerned, *Good Feeling* was 'a cracking record but the timing just wasn't right or something; it didn't connect with anybody.'

The next thing to do after recording an album, of course, is to promote it – and if you want to get to the maximum number of people in the shortest possible time, you can't do much better than tour as special guests of the biggest band in the land. In 1997, as they remain today, that was Oasis – and Travis were the lucky lads who got the all-important Noel nod. Their invitation to play ten dates to an estimated 100,000 people was a happy accident that sprung from a human tragedy that might almost have inspired Fran to put pen to lyrical paper.

The release of 'All I Want To Do Is Rock' had turned a few industry heads, but none more agreeable than Leo Finlay. The young Irishman was A&R editor at *Music Week*, the one publication everyone in the business reads, and was keen to give the band an early chance to get their name in print. 'We hung out for an afternoon,' Doug recalls, 'and he was really into the whole spirit of the band. A few days later we went off to work on the album and then, just before Christmas, we found out that he was dead... it was *devastating*.'

Finlay had a wife and family in Dublin who needed support, and a number of bands who'd warmed to his enthusiastic nature agreed to play a benefit gig for his dependents. Travis were quick to volunteer their services, even though they'd only met Leo once, but could hardly have imagined the spin-off their warm-heartedness would inspire. Noel Gallagher had been invited to the gig by *Melody Maker* writer Paul Mathur, the evening's master of ceremonies, and popped in to lend support just as Travis took the stage. Their set was, in Mathur's words, 'ragged and occasionally thrilling... the bad bits were bravely over-ambitious, the good bits twinkled with promise.'

Maybe it was the twinkling that stayed with Noel, because the next place he was seen parking his Rolls-Royce was outside the 100 Club in Oxford Street where Travis were playing a two-night stand.

Bass player Colin Greenwood from Radiohead had also attended the benefit gig, along with producer Nigel Godrich. When the former approached Fran and congratulated him on the set, Mr Healy didn't even recognise him! Later he met up with Nigel Godrich and drowned his blushes… the pair hitting it off so well that Nigel would be in the frame for producing the band's second album a year and a half later.

Before heading out on the road with Manchester's finest, Travis had a date to keep at New York's CMJ festival, an annual junket of movers and shakers within the American record business. The mood was appreciably upbeat, and they were happily imbibing the best that room service had to offer while enjoying late-night TV screenings of classic horror films and occasionally considering the live performance that was the reason for them being in the Big Apple.

'We can be brilliant, or the worst band in the world, but we're never boring'.

You could forgive their confidence, having played as many times as they now had – but unpredictability was part of their charm. 'We can be brilliant, or the worst band in the world,' said Fran, 'but we're never boring'. True to form, they then went on to play a perfectly adequate gig. It turned out they'd been booked to play two nights, the first at a promotional party for Epic Records (the label that would release their music in the States) where they had to play second fiddle to a home-based crew rejoicing in the name of Furball.

Even though they didn't rate it one of their greatest gigs, *Melody Maker*'s Paul Mathur (there to cover the event) was especially impressed by Andy's approach to playing the guitar. 'Half the time he looks at his instrument like it's just gone off in his hand, or he's woken up to find himself holding some weird wood and string thing, the purpose of which eludes him. The rest of the time he braids feisty guitar lines around Travis's prismatic pop. While lighting a cigarette.'

Andy certainly enlivened a stage presence that sometimes bordered on the static. Still, why should rock be lumbered with clichés? After all, while in New York they spotted 1970s rock icon Lou Reed - an influence on everybody from David Bowie to Marilyn Manson - not in a limo... but on a bicycle!

The anthemic 'Tied To The 90s' was selected as their next single release, emerging in early August and reaching a highest chart position of 30 – far and away the best showing to date. Bonus tracks were as ever in evidence, including 'City In The Rain', 'Whenever She Comes Around', 'Standing On My Own' and 'Me Beside You'.

The Oasis *Be Here Now* Tour in September 1997 had clearly been a turning point for the band. To have the public seal of approval from Britain's most popular band was mind-blowing enough, even before Liam started bashing a tambourine in the wings to 'All I Want To Do... ', a number he called 'my fuckin' favourite singin' song.'

Yet it had all seemed so different on Saturday, 13 September at 7.30pm as they prepared to go on stage at the Point, Exeter. 'We weren't nervous at all,' Fran explained afterwards. 'We just stood there. The house lights were on. There was a guy holding open this massive curtain, and then the lights went down. The crowd sounded like an aeroplane taking off. Screaming and clapping. Oasis and their whole entourage stood on the steps at the side, watching us do our first gig. I was so calm it kind of freaked me out because I was so unfazed by it.'

Dougie could feel the energy coming off the audience 'like a hair-raising fireball,' while Andy, as down to earth as ever, found it less nerve-wracking than playing to ten people. But even the seen-it-all Dougie got off on what he called the 'Queen moment' of the set – 7,000 people clapping along to 'Good Feeling.' The real pay-off came the following day while record-shopping in the town centre before the second Exeter gig when the band were recognised by three Oasis fans who saw them play the night before - they had just been out especially to buy the Travis album.

The media spotlight was very much on this tour, the biggest of the autumn, and Travis found themselves the subject of many more column inches than they'd ever previously enjoyed. *Sky* magazine, for instance, gave their opening pair of gigs a rapturous review which gives a taste of their fast-maturing stage presence: 'Where many support bands blink apologetically in the glare of the sweeping spotlights, Travis revel in their illumination. The fans nod along to the barnstormers and burn their fingers on lighters during the ballads. They aren't merely tolerating a necessary interminable support band. They're enjoying it, loving it... the jet-powered roar for Travis is approaching the volume of the scream when Oasis take the stage.'

'My mum didn't get a chance to do what she wanted in life, so she's always encouraged me to do exactly what I wanted.'

The gig at Manchester's cavernous GMEX Arena was, of course, Oasis's hometown date on their tour. Even so, Noel Gallagher was happy to ensure the spotlight was shared around a bit, taking it upon himself to take the stage and add guitar to 'All I Want To Do Is Rock'. The resulting noise would be made available to a wider audience as a bonus track when the 'More Than Us' EP was released the following March.

Touring proved a wearing experience for Travis – and though you might have understood them becoming just a *little* frayed while trying to keep up with the headliners' noted excess, the truth was just a little more prosaic. Dougie caught influenza, Andy got a cyst, and Fran tore a ligament in his elbow. This, he explained, was more serious than it seemed in terms of the Travis stage act. 'It really hurts me when I punch the air in 'Tied To The 90s', but I can't sing that song without doing it.' He wouldn't last the week without a visit to London's Harley Street for an injection to ease the pain, flying up to Aberdeen a day later than his colleagues.

And Aberdeen was to be a very special gig indeed. Saturday 20 September at the E&CC was, Andy admitted, 'the date we're most nervous about' – because the band's families were coming to see them play. All acknowledged the parts their parents' support had played in helping them get this far, especially Fran. 'My mum didn't get a chance to do what she wanted in life,' says Fran. 'So she's always encouraged me to do exactly what I wanted.' Her pride can only be imagined... and she was to be seen backstage after chatting away with the Gallaghers' mother, Peggy, as if they'd known each other all their lives.

'He went off on one, telling me it's like John Lennon and that I should ride a penny farthing in the video.'

Patronage from Oasis had proved useful to the Verve, whose Richard Ashcroft had been the subject of 'Cast No Shadow', and if Travis hadn't been immortalised in song they had plenty of their own to contribute. Fran played some of his works in progress to Liam backstage, including a song called 'Luv' he'd written a couple of years earlier when his girlfriend had dumped him en route to university. 'He went off on one, telling me it's like John Lennon and that I should ride a penny farthing in the video.'

Liam took a demo tape away and returned, red-eyed and obviously moved, some while later. Apparently, when Bonehead (guitarist Paul Arthurs) heard it, his reaction was similar. Travis and

Oasis had, Fran reflected, got a lot in common. 'We appeal to ordinary people, not just students, because what we both are is fundamentally a bunch of mates.'

Meanwhile, back in the Len Wright Sleeper Coach, rapper Snoop Doggy Dogg, super Swedes Abba and the Beatles' *Red* compilation (1962-66) vied for position on the CD player. And 'Happy', released in October, became the forth single from *Good Feeling*, its modest No. 38 peak suggesting that most people had by now bought the album. Bonus tracks on the formats for those who invested included 'Unbelievers' and 'Everyday Faces' (CD1) and 'When I'm Feeling Blue (Days of the Week)' and 'Mother' (CD2). The 'Happy' video had been filmed in the States as recently as the previous month, Travis having flown out there at the end of the Oasis tour.

The penultimate month of 1997 saw the quartet back on the other side of the Atlantic, enjoying their first taste of life on tour in the States, opening for the excellent Ben Folds Five in venues ranging from the legendary Fillmore ballroom in San Francisco, from whose stage psychedelic music took off to dominate the rock world in the late 1960s, to smaller venues like the Club Caprice on Redondo Beach where you almost expected the stage to be separated from the crowd by wire mesh, Blues Brothers style.

They may have taken their name from a character in the film *Paris, Texas*, but Travis were certainly foreigners abroad as far as the great American populace were concerned. Some fans would gladly have paid just to hear them talk in their 'quaint' Scottish voices. Those accents were greeted with shouts of 'Sean Connery!' and '*Trainspotting*!' by those mildly acquainted with their home country's culture, but thankfully there were those – including the family of Dougie's American girlfriend, Justina – who related to Travis on a rather more meaningful level.

The last week of the tour saw the band flying out their nearest and dearest to do some West Coast sightseeing and pre-Christmas shopping as things wound down: Fran declared his mother's arrival the biggest event of the tour: 'I don't care how un-rock 'n' roll it

seems, but she's done a lot for me and the band.'

It had indeed been an eventful tour, one of the highlights of which had been in Cleveland: it had snowed and they hadn't got on stage until one in the morning, while Dougie enjoyed a 25-hour 25th birthday thanks to a handily placed time zone. Texas had been an eye-opener in more ways than one, Fran enjoying his first taste of horse riding and Dougie having to dodge the crack salesmen operating outside a launderette next to their hotel. All this added a new resonance to the 'U16 Girls' lyric about meeting a girl in LA - at the time of writing the song, Fran had never been near the place. Now life had imitated art.

Having charmed the Yanks, it was back to Blighty for a quick tour, which peaked at London's Astoria on 23 January with support from Unbelievable Truth, the Hybirds and Ultrasound. 'Their smooth waters seem shallow at first glance,' read one typical review, 'but they have depths of Lake Titicaca proportions. Fran's charismatic, winning half-smirk (the one he shares with Jon Bon Jovi) accompanies everything they do and implies he knows things you don't. Like just how good Travis are.'

After a well-earned break, Travis's next port of call was to be a very special one – playing their home town's renowned Barrowlands Ballroom, known affectionately as 'The Barras'. They performed alongside Celtic cousins Catatonia and Edinburgh's own Idlewild on the Radio 1-sponsored *Evening Session* Tour (the jaunt also took in Manchester University, the Birmingham Irish Centre and Newport Centre).

This long-awaited homecoming show would be a nerve-racking one for all concerned, and not merely because Travis's families were represented in force on a hugely extended guest list. Not only was it the first time they'd played live for two months – they decided not to rehearse – Fran, who'd been unwell the previous day with a stomach upset, suffered an attack of diarrhoea five songs into the set. 'I did have to kneel down at one point... ' Dougie: 'That's so we could scoop out his pants.' Having survived that scare, he charmed the assembled Glaswegian hordes by dedicating 'I Love You Anyways' to his mum.

Select magazine's Neil Mason, who was reviewing the gig, noted that Cerys 'managed to upset a thousand or so Glaswegians by innocently asking "who won the rugby?" And, as Travis take to the stage, guitar player Andy Dunlop's mum adds to the Travis mum legend by almost finding herself on the stage after being misdirected out of the dressing room!' Fran's mum, for her part, became great friends with Cerys backstage.

DJ Steve Lamacq, a long-time champion of the Travis cause, pronounced the tour 'bloody brilliant – I never want to go home.' As well as the bands playing live each night, sessions recorded in the afternoons on the bus added to the diversity. Prior to the Glasgow gig, seven-piece Belle and Sebastian appeared to play a new song, 'Wrong Love', for the assembled populace (and a nation of listeners).

In Newport, it was the turn of another set of local heroes, 60 Ft Dolls, to busk away, this time as a duo on acoustic guitar and shakers, before Lamacq, who'd lost track of time completely, rushed from bus to stage to introduce Idlewild. He explained why he chose Travis as members of his élite equipe. 'Because we were booking this tour in November, we wanted to get bands we thought were going to come through. I met them in New York at the CMJ festival. They're the kind of band you'd like to go on tour with because they're really nice to hang around with. Chipper tunes, too.'

Andy and the inimitable Cerys hit it off to such an extent that he sold her a small Spanish classical guitar he'd bought it for a tenner just days earlier (he doubled his money). It gave the Catatonia chanteuse the chance to re-visit the folk songs she used to sing as a busker.

Fran, Cerys and Catatonia guitarist, Mark would often be found relaxing together in the lounge at the back of the bus, while the Barrowlands show had seen Cerys moshing down the front. Travis's fast-rising stock could be measured by the queues of autograph-hunters at the door of the tour bus, including a startling number of girls who wanted body parts signed...

The *More Than Us* EP, released in 30 March 1998, was an interesting beast. It showcased the track from the first album that had been orchestrated by Anne Dudley, and here 're-strung' by the same source, but also brought several more collaborative ventures to the table. 'Give Me Some Truth' was a John Lennon rant from 1971's classic *Imagine* album, also covered recently by Ash. 'All I Want to Do Is Rock' was the previously mentioned GMEX performance with additional guitar from Noel Gallagher. The last track of *Good Feeling* completed the first CD, but not in its original form. This version of 'Funny Thing' had been specially recorded at Mayfair Studios in London's Primrose Hill with Tim Simenon, the Bomb The Bass artist and producer who was another client of Animal Management. 'A new dance direction?' shrugged Fran. 'Not really. I was out having a drink one night and got talking to him...'

'You can never complain about people being interested in you, no publicity is bad publicity.'

The second disc paired the title track with a demo version of a new song, 'More Than Us' played acoustic-style on Italian radio, 'Beautiful Bird', 'Reason' (with Susie Hug) and – last but not least – three postcards of chairs and one of Travis!

It was set to be a busy summer for Travis. Aside from playing Glasgow's Garage in May (when Fran curiously forgot the words to long-time but unrecorded stage favourite 'She's So Strange'), they were confirmed as headliners for the Bude Rock festival in Cornwall, with Catatonia, 60ft Dolls, Space, Carrie and Ether among the other acts playing. July found them at Phoenix '98 at Long Marston Airfield, and, for the second year running, at T In The Park. The sun shone at the latter as they took to the stage, opening with 'All I Want To Do Is Rock' and receiving the reception returning heroes deserve – not surprising, since they were the only Scottish band playing the main stage that day.

Having played a festival in Venice the previous day, Travis had been stranded at the airport due to airline complications. Landing in London at 2am rather than the scheduled 9.30pm, the band grabbed a few hours' sleep before the 6am flight to Edinburgh. A coach drive to the festival site took three times as long as it should, thanks to being misdirected by stewards – and, once backstage, Radio One and STV wanted their pound of flesh as if they were bright eyed and bushy-tailed. 'You can never complain about people being interested in you,' announced a more than reasonable Douglas. 'No publicity is bad publicity.'

While T In The Park had become something of a fixture in the Travis calendar – the previous year they played in a tent, now they were playing the main stage – the jewel in the summer crown was a headline slot on the *Melody Maker* Stage at Reading Festival on Saturday 29 August. Once a heavy metal festival, the Bank Holiday event was enjoying a revival as the most prestigious event of the season, with all the biggest names.

'Why Does It Always Rain On Me?', a song with a big chorus and amusing lyrics destined to become a classic, was previewed at that gig, a real triumph for the band. 'As You Are' was another song previewed at the festivals during the summer, while the *Melody Maker* reviewer at Reading reckoned Travis was 'the reason people congregate in fields every summer. This is *festive*...'

Fran was knocked out at how many fans were joining in. 'It's nice to see more people knowing the songs. At the end of 'All I Want To Do Is Rock' 'cos when we finish the song quietly, and you can hear people singing it, and you're hearing them and you're like, 'My God'. It's weird. It's strange cos when you're sitting down and you're writing stuff, you never think that, you really don't. You write it just because it sounds good...'

CHAPTER SEVEN

THE MEN WHO...

Received wisdom has it the second album is a testing time for any group. Having showcased the best songs they had written over several years of trying, the sophomore band often struggle to maintain the quality and creativity that caused interest in them in the first instance. This is often exacerbated by months and months of touring before being expected to fly straight back to the studio to start on the follow-up. The poor songwriter is already examining his first album cast-offs, having been too exhausted to come up with any half-decent pop songs, the bassist and drummer have fallen out on the road and the lead guitarist's acquired some of the exceedingly strange habits that come hand-in-hand with overnight fame. Add to which the fact that they're all still on £100-a-week as the royalties have yet to filter through, and it's little wonder the best most people hope for from a second album is something approaching a carbon copy of the first.

Not so Travis, in any respect. Fran Healy was well aware of the pitfalls. When *Select* magazine spoke to him at the end of 1998 for a preview of the major releases for the coming year, he quipped: 'You know what they say, you get 24 months to record your first album and six months to do your second... ' He unashamedly confessed that he was reviewing his back pages and 'some of the songs are from years ago. I used to think that you could only use songs that were less than a month old or something, but when I realised people like Paul McCartney and REM release songs they wrote years before, I decided it was okay.'

'At the end of the first album we thought we were magic when we were pure rubbish. It's not changed. It's just that maybe we've got a wee bit better.'

At this point, Fran was buoyant about an album that had originally rejoiced in the working title of *Final Times*. This came from a newspaper seller he'd often encountered in the centre of Glasgow on Argyll Street, who'd inhabited the pitch outside Marks & Spencer for 'about 100 years.' Fran used to think his late-edition clarion call was 'a bit heavy. I thought of using that [as a title], what with the end of the millennium and all that, but decided it was a bit too ominous.'

The title eventually selected, *The Man Who*, was derived from Oliver Sacks' book on schizophrenia, *The Man Who Mistook His Wife*

For A Hat. The reason, apparently, was the number of reviews for the first album that had labelled Travis a schizophrenic band, so 'a well-thumbed compendium of schizophrenic case studies' (as the official website explained it) was selected to lend its name.

Fran admitted the album they were recording was considerably more mature than its predecessor, and invited critics to listen to the last song on *Good Feeling* and the first track of *The Man Who* to see the link. This would be more of a song album than a rock album, 'an album for staying in rather than going out.' He denied absolutely that the band had changed tack. 'At the end of the first album we thought we were magic when we were pure rubbish. It's not changed. It's just that maybe we've got a wee bit better.'

Even after they'd settled on a name for the album, recording it was going to be far from plain sailing. They put the finished product together from sessions with two producers; Mike Hedges and Nigel Godrich. Though the latter had worked with the likes of REM, Beck and Pavement there was no doubt he was best known for his work with Radiohead. The quartet clearly now felt they were beyond the comparisons, though Fran admitted the choice of Godrich was opening the door to future derogatory comments.

Worse still, during the sessions Fran decided some of the songs chosen just didn't fit, so retired to his garret to write some more. This from a man who 'absolutely hates' the process. Days came and went, turning into weeks, and many a false dawn was seen. Three songs were deleted in one swoop, and the pressure and stress was piling high on Fran's shoulders. But the last two songs of this fresh batch, 'Writing To Reach You' and 'Driftwood', more than justified his decision. 'You just let the songs come by themselves and try not to touch them,' he later explained. 'I'm sick of hearing records that sound like they've been fiddled with too much.'

Dougie, for one, was feeling the pressure just as much, largely because he wished he could pen a song to ease his friend's burden. Fran, for his part, even asked Andy Macdonald to start dropping round at his flat in north London's trendy Muswell Hill suburb on a regular basis every Wednesday at 1 o'clock 'to crack the whip and get me to do a bit of work. Andy would come down: "Give me your songs." And sometimes I wouldn't have any.'

It had all started so well, when in the spirit of European Union, band and producer Hedges had decamped across the Channel to a country house in Normandy which had been converted into a studio. It was nothing short of an idyllic setting, and the band were delighted to work with a 'master who specialises in perfect pop'. What was more significant from their record company's point of view, perhaps, is that Hedges had presided over the last two Manic Street Preachers albums which had turned the Welsh indie guitar-rockers into a megaband.

The sessions were to last between 4 and 24 June, and to begin with at least progress was nothing short of perfect. They sat on the open veranda watching shooting stars before retiring, then next morning strolled down to Hedges' abode in the grounds to breakfast agreeably on croissants and discuss what was to be achieved in the coming day. They were following in some well-known footsteps: examination of the high scores on the pinball machine revealed JDB – a certain Mr Bradfield – to have posted the three to beat. 'The best we could do was knock him off second spot.'

The desk in Hedges' chateau was the one Pink Floyd used to record *Dark Side Of The Moon*, and made everything sound as warm, which helped as the cellar studio – a converted wine cellar with stone walls – was cold and clammy. A small camera in the corner gave Mike a visual reference, the only other means of communication being via vocal microphones. Upstairs, in complete contrast, a piano sat in a ballroom with sunlight streaming in through the south-facing window. 'I wrote a song called "Flowers In The Window" on this piano when the sun shone,' said Fran, who also admitted to cracking one of the centuries-old pieces of glass with a Frisbee when outside!

Then the Hedges sessions just ended. 'We got some really good performances with Mike,' said label head Macdonald, 'but he had other obligations. It's no disrespect to him at all, but there's something very special about the relationship they have with Nigel.' The shaven-headed Godrich, at age 28, was very much a contemporary of the band compared with the rather more senior Hedges, who had also worked (pre-Manics) with Banshees spin-offs the Creatures, the Cure and the Cult. He himself was quoted as saying his work with the Manics had left him 'knackered'.

On the plus side, the band would re-cross the channel with five songs in their baggage, three of which would make it onto the final album: 'She's So Strange', 'Why Does It Always Rain On Me?' and 'Turn', all of which would be remixed (or 'fucked up' in Godrich-speak) at Mayfair Studios to fit more closely with the vibe of the remainder. The tie-up with Godrich was a fascinating one given the critics' infamous Radiohead references when Travis had come on the scene. They'd met him at the same benefit gig that Noel Gallagher had dropped in on, and kept in touch – in fact, he'd been one of the first names in the frame. He'd certainly help Travis take their sound to new dimensions.

Their first experience of him had come before their trip to France, at RAK Studios in May 1998, adding impromptu backing vocals to former bill-sharers Ultrasound's 'Stay Young'. They were fascinated at how he was managing to get everything to sound so clear, crediting him with 'ears like a bat'. His work with Travis would span six months and as many studios before the difficult second album was at last complete.

Apart from his sonic abilities, Godrich's best attribute was to lull Travis into a sense of false security, knowing that they tended to freeze when the red 'recording' light came on - so he'd keep everything very informal. But when it came down to the finished product, everything would be present and correct, panned neatly left, right and centre.

... And what an album they had delivered. The record opened with 'Writing To Reach You', one of the last two songs to be written but one that had been kicking around since December 1995.

Fran's described it as 'Kafka's *Letters To Felice*-meets-Oasis', and revealed it had its genesis back in the old days in Glasgow when he was living in a cold water flat. 'It was about minus 22 degrees, two fires going and I was getting fuzzy-headed because the windows were frozen shut.' Having had the idea kicking around for three years or so, he finished it off in twenty minutes. The letters in question, by the way, were all written to a woman Kafka had hardly met. 'I don't read a lot,' says Fran, 'but those letters were amazing.'

Another Scottish band, Del Amitri, was possibly the best musical reference point here, while the lyrics peaked with Fran's side-mention of the Oasis track 'Wonderwall'. Ironically, Dougie met Liam Gallagher in the street during a break from recording and invited him to the studio: "Writing'... was the song being worked on when Liam finally appeared, and the bass player was worried about how he'd react to the reference. Fran would later explain it wasn't so much biting the hand that fed them as a way of drawing people in. 'I'm pleased we managed to draw on Kafka and Oasis in the same song.'

No change of pace for 'The Fear', but the season had morphed into autumn, a time of change, and the fear is a fear of change. The fading, repeating line is eventually drowned out by a whooshing sound... the winter wind biting around the ankles perhaps? This, along with the later 'Luv', was the nearest to offering a chance for Radiohead comparisons that had so dogged their earlier career. That said, the original demo had apparently sounded more like hoary old blues-rockers Led Zeppelin! Having decided corporately to approach it 'more gently', Travis gave it a couple of tentative runs through – but unknown to them, while they were rehearsing Godrich was recording. After something like the fifth try, they agreed they were ready to go for 'a take', only to get the message in their headphones that recording was already complete!

'The Fear' was in fact a key track on the album, despite having been written by Fran a year before they got their record deal. His fear had been that his then girlfriend was about to chuck him, but for

Dougie the song represented much more. 'If there's an underlying theme to this album, it's that you shouldn't be afraid to be vulnerable. 'The Fear' reflects that.'

'As You Are' immediately sent you reaching for your Beatles CDs – almost Paul McCartney singing 'Across The Universe' (which is strange because it's a Lennon song!). Could the title be a reference to Nirvana, and 'Come As You Are'? Certainly it builds to an intense mid-section, with the Healy voice soaring and grating before a bit of melodic bass-work (McCartney's influence again?) led to a sterling electric guitar lick introducing the last verse. By this time, the song and the album had well and truly plugged in; there's a definite feeling of progression.

Fran has since traced the title back not to Kurt Cobain but to a poem he was given by an old man on a train from Birmingham to Glasgow in 1983. Returning home from his auntie's house, young Fran was being naughty – and, seeing his mother's annoyance, a gentleman in the same carriage decided to intervene. He played with the kid, kept him entertained and at the end of the journey gave them a poem on a piece of paper: "As you are now/So once was I/ Remember this, as time goes by/As I am now/Soon you will be/ Remember this and pray for me." Fran recounted this story to his manager one day and then the penny dropped - *that's* where 'As You Are' had come from. 'I hadn't even thought about it… '

Next up came 'Driftwood', the most musically uptempo (yet utterly melancholy) offering so far, with its scurrying folk-guitar strum, but again there's a feeling of restraint. The melody had come to Fran while he was washing dishes – but when he revisited the tape he'd made he thought he'd taped over it. Only in the last thirty seconds did the catchy chorus appear, but that was enough.

You could almost imagine 1960s singer-songwriter Donovan tackling this one, though the *New Musical Express* album review invoked the memory of Roddy Frame's equally canny Scots, Aztec Camera, in their *High Land, Hard Rain* period. The lyric found Fran having fun with the words; with a tune to die for, there seemed every chance that Fran's creation would soon be on the airwaves. Certainly, long before release, Neil had dubbed this 'Radio song of the fucking year'... would time prove him right?

Five songs in, 'The Last Laugh Of The Laughter' added a piano to the mix and sent Fran into a higher-pitched, almost female delivery. And that's no surprise, since the original demo had a French lady hairdresser singing. Fran had written the song while on holiday in Israel. A party of hairdressers were staying in his hotel, and he came up with this while on a boat trip. They supplied the alternate-line translations and even performed on the demo: 'She was singing it better than me,' insisted the ever-modest writer. Not all reviewers agreed, *Guitarist* magazine reckoning the track 'reminds you why you're praying Simon and Garfunkel never reform...'

If vinyl albums still existed, we'd now be turning the record over. Interestingly, three of the five 'Side Two' tracks stemmed from the Chateau de la Rouge Motte sessions, kicking off with 'Turn'. Described by Fran as 'a list of wishes', it dated back to the time he spent at Millport which had seen him come up with several other major songs, including 'All I Want To Do Is Rock'. Electric guitar, unusually, makes itself felt from the start – none of the usual slow build here – and the end result is definitely an epic rock song.

The Byrds had a hit a quarter of a century earlier with 'Turn Turn Turn', a song which took its words from the biblical book of Ecclesiastes, courtesy of folk singer Pete Seeger. Perhaps Fran was inspired by the song, and indeed some of his own lines contain a certain religious resonance.

Next up, mysteriously dedicated 'for NK', was 'Why Does It Always Rain On Me?', another Chateau cut whose shambling rhythm continued the more upbeat mood of the second 'side'. It was a song that had been finished in Israel, on the same trip that had yielded 'The Last Laugh Of The Laughter', but had begun life in Madrid where Fran had been holed up doing press for the first album. The common denominator between Spain and Israel was rain, surprising for holiday locations but grist to the songwriter's mill.

While in Madrid, he'd been depressed at *Good Feeling*'s rapid descent from the UK charts, and felt people back home were concealing the truth from him so as not to put him off his lonely job peddling the band to a country which was hardly aware of them. That said, he came up with something one reviewer neatly described as 'the paranoid musical comedown to 'Itchycoo Park'... ' and indeed it did share the lolloping gait of the Small Faces' summer anthem if not its Cockney optimism. One reviewer detected a homage to Jeff Buckley, late son of the late (and even greater) Tim.

There was a temptation to play the song at a faster, sprightlier tempo, but Travis resisted this as they felt some of the emotional impact would be lost. Having passed the taxi driver's test, they knew in Fran's words that 'This could be one of those tunes that people will jump on... the title is a memorable line as well, which definitely helped.'

A low-key, distinctly Dylan-esque harmonica introduced 'Luv', a song that bemoans an affair that's reached an end for the other partner. The inspiration here came when Fran's ex-girlfriend left Glasgow for St. Andrews University, leaving him in misery. He even sent her a demo of the song to express his feelings, though when they met again at Christmas she denied receiving it 'but I knew it had got to her'. She'd have had to be hard-hearted not to have shed the odd tear...

The spelling of the title suggested a nod to John Lennon, while Anne (Art Of Noise) Dudley's involvement drew an obvious comparison with the first album's 'More Than Us'. The track faded out after five melancholy minutes with guitar feedback echoing the opening harmonica – a neat way to end a song with many emotional rough edges.

'She's So Strange' was the third and final track from the Mike Hedges sessions and arrested from the start – a cold vocal introduction introducing some very direct, not to say bizarre, imagery of cats sniffing glue and girls with moustaches. Reminiscent of the Bluetones' finest moment from '96, 'Slight Return', but downplayed by several degrees, it could have been Blur, Bowie or the Beatles (was that a 'Paperback Writer' reference in the lyric?).

The song was probably the oldest of all of them recorded on the album, schoolfriend Robert Elliott having recalled Glass Onion playing it back in the Glasgow club days. Its inspiration was Janet Leigh's character which enjoyed 45 minutes of fame in Alfred Hitchcock's classic horror film *Psycho* – who can forget the shower scene? – while the first chord Fran plays was one he came across by accident in a musical instrument shop while buying a 12-string guitar... and liked it so much he kept both!

The relatively brief ten tracks was designed to leave the public wanting more, and 'Slide Show' ended proceedings on a suitably final note with the sound of a closing car door. It seemed likely to be a long farewell, too, with the CD timing counter reading 10 minutes 31 seconds, but a strummed acoustic guitar suggested no great pomp and circumstance.

This was a song Fran wrote during a solo session (with sandwiches and sleeping bag, this is a boy who comes prepared for anything) in the Kings Cross, London, rehearsal rooms Travis used. Lyrical sideswipes were again in evidence, with the Manic Street Preachers ('Design For Life'), Beck ('Devil's Haircut') and Oasis ('Wonderwall' again) coming into focus. Its writer claimed the point was to explain how songs can 'bookmark events in your life', and admits to having run into Noel Gallagher the day he wrote it.

They originally tried to record the song while driving around London's St John's Wood, the neighbourhood where RAK studios was situated, but gave up and instead decided they'd mix in some street-level sound effects using Neil's car. More door-slamming brings things to a conclusion after three and a half minutes... only for guitar feedback to break the silence three minutes and 14 seconds later and rouse any unsuspecting listener who might have been lulled into a reverie.

'The Blue Flashing Light' is a wake-up call in more ways than one, taking you into the heart of a man destined to spend his Saturday night alone knowing that awful things are taking place next door – in its writer's words, 'the attitude people have – it's none of our business until something terrible happens.' Clashing electric guitar chords and some remarkably violent lyrics, certainly compared with the rest of the album, make this a terrifying proposition. 'It started out as a song about my friend's brother. But the lyric was rubbish, so I wrote it from the perspective of someone who is a witness to domestic violence of some kind. I imagined them looking out their window but yet feeling that they can't do anything to help.'

It was written and recorded after the rest of the album, when B-sides were being considered, but made such an impact with those who heard it that the band were implored to put it on. Reasoning – rightly – that it would 'blow the whole continuity of gentleness', Fran compromised and included it as a secret track which must have caused havoc at many a middle-class dinner party! 'It still scares the shit out of me,' confessed its composer, 'because I forget it's there.'

Dougie had lobbied hard for its inclusion, but conceded it wouldn't have sat in the album proper as it is. He'd always loved *Nevermind* by Nirvana, and recalls 'getting it, taking it home, putting it on in my bedroom and hoping that maybe there'll be an extra song, and then there is and you think: "Oh yes you beauty!" So it's cool.'

'It's quite a gentle record – very organic – so we wanted a cover to reflect that.'

The singing on this album had been particularly impressive, Fran revealing that his voice had still been 'settling' when he joined the band, and that he expected to peak between the ages of 30 and 32. Design-wise, there was little doubt the sleeve had been created by (or for) art students. Nine of the 12 booklet pages were devoid of typography, all lyrics and credits being printed in minuscule white type on the grey background of pages 10 and 11. It was also dedicated to recently deceased film-maker Stanley Kubrick... oh, and 'Shirley'.

The cover itself just bore the band name and title, again in shades of grey, with the four members standing in a snow-swept field, well-insulated against the cold. Fran gave the music to an art company called Blue Source and told them to come up with a concept that matched. 'It's quite a gentle record – very organic – so we wanted a cover to reflect that.' They listened to it and decided that the best place to go was somewhere that was quite untouched. For Dougie, it was important to go somewhere unidentifiable because the band believe 'music has no geography.'

Travis had taken time out of recording and mixing sessions to fly up to the Scottish highland ski resort of Aviemore for the January '99 photo shoot – as close a banker as you could get for snow. Unfortunately, they were greeted by rain and high winds, and it seemed they'd fly back without the desired shot. Lo and behold, someone up there must have been a Travis fan, as they were pulled out of their beds at 5.30am in the morning to pose among a brand new snowfall. For Fran, 'the landscape is second to none... though the ski resort needs some seeing to.'

'When you're small and fancy someone, instead of kissing them you hit them.'

The coats were the models' own, as they say in the *Vogue* small print, except for Dougie whose fur-collared job was considered 'a little too retro, a little too Echo and the Bunnymen'. He borrowed one from a record company worker. After all was done and dusted, someone had the temerity to ask whether it was suitable for an album released in May to have a snowy colour. 'In the summer it's sand, in the winter it's snow' came the instant reply. As far as Fran was concerned, the result was 'one of the best bits of art work of the year.'

A foot would be dipped back into the water of live performance on 24 February at King's College in London. The jungle drums had ensured the student population was augmented by a large number of dyed-in-the-wool Travis fans, for a set that daringly kicked off with a song unfamiliar to all – 'Village Man'. Then came three tracks from the as-yet unheard album before the first album's familiar 'The Line Is Fine'. Next up was 'Blue On A Black Weekend', another B-side (this time from the 'All I Want To Do Is Rock' single) which was greeted with much delight.

This was followed by an acoustic interlude during which Andy, Neil and Dougie left the stage for a well-earned break. The next song, 'Only Molly Knows', was preceded by a monologue from its writer explaining how it was inspired by his friend Lesley's three year old son, Jack, who showed affection for his 'girlfriend' Molly in an aggressive way. 'When you're small and fancy someone,' he explained, 'instead of kissing them you hit them. I wrote the songs so he could give it to her when he's 20.' Again, it was a great song that would almost be thrown away as a B-side.

Another so far unheard song, the France-inspired 'Flowers In The Window', was played when the missing trio returned, along with more material from the forthcoming album, but the encore reverted to a teaming of tried and tested *Good Feeling* favourites in 'Good Day To Die' and the energetic 'Happy'.

Ironically given the crowd's reception, press reviews of the gig were decidedly downbeat. 'All I Want To Do Is Dadrock' screamed the *New Musical Express* headline, next to a picture of Fran captioned 'a Travis-ty'. Yet reviewer Mark Beaumont, who'd interviewed the band in past months, seemed to feel that some sacred bond between him and his favourite band had been broken, hoped-for favourites not played and new songs introduced that lacked the 'Stupid Factor' of half of *Good Feeling*. 'Travis played 11 new songs tonight,' ran the concluding sentence. 'Sometimes, it seems, The Tunes are not enough.'

The effect of such criticism – forgettable tunes, commercially reprogrammed, genetically engineered to sell Nissan Micras and more – could have been devastating on a band about to release an album on which so many hopes rested. Indeed, one fellow musician described them as the nastiest reviews he'd ever read. Yet according to Independiente's Tony Crean, it only made the band redouble their studio efforts. 'This spurred the band to work really hard to give the album a live feel, which really paid off.'

Interestingly, the set-opening 'Village Man' had been tagged to appear on the album as late as February, Fran describing it as the 'one all-out rock song on it', but its fate was to be shuffled off to become a mere bonus track on the 'Why Does It Always Rain On Me?' single. Given all the promising songs that wouldn't make it to album, a collection of B-sides and bonuses similar to Oasis's 'Masterplan' seemed a highly likely project in the months/years to come.

'Frannie won't show us any of his bad songs; he's his own worst critic.'

Andy thought the high quality of these extra tracks was because 'Frannie won't show us any of his bad songs; he's his own worst critic.' Dougie recalled the craze in the 1980s of instrumental B-sides. 'It's a rip off. It's just nice for people who are buying the songs to get quality!'

Andy liked the idea that 'when you thought you knew a band, you had their two albums and then you heard a song and you didn't know where it was from, there was a sudden excitement of fishing out that song.' Dougie: 'I remember buying Suede's first single, and buying the 12-inch, and the B-side was just astonishing, it was brilliant!'

Reviews of the album would be decidedly mixed, and most of the magazines which nominated it as their 'Record of the Year' come the millennium's end must have been hoping their readers didn't have long memories. There were parallels with Oasis's second album *(What's The Story) Morning Glory*, which had in its time been lambasted as 'more of the same' only to confound the critics by passing the only real acid test – public acceptance – with flying colours.

Danny Eccleston of *Q* magazine, who'd so memorably fallen in love with *Good Feeling*, was one of many who couldn't cope with the fact that this was an altogether more introspective affair that took its cues from the softer side of the debut. He felt it promised much with the opening quartet, 'four peerless songs: languid, pushed along on sad-eyed acoustic guitars and uncoiling like snakes, bringing hints of depression, disorientation and stagnation.' Then, as he saw it, the momentum was lost. 'Six months of recording seems to have planed off the peaks and purged anything garish, rocking or funny/knowing – as if Travis were told that the most enchanting aspects of *Good Feeling* were childish things to be put away.'

Fortunately, secretive 'Blue Flashing Light' got the thumbs-up. 'A vivid Glaswegian tableau of domestic violence and adolescent helplessness, spat out by a bug-eyed and unignorable Healy, it could so easily have been the pivot and the passionate core of an even better record.' Two out of five...

Guitar magazine's Patrick Jennings was more generous with four stars, deeming this somewhat poetically 'the perfect accompaniment to rainy summer afternoons. Or just when it's raining in your heart.' He highlighted 'As You Are' for Andy Dunlop's gentle weeps and moans in the background. Four stars were the reward for 'good songwriters not trying too hard. So no, they don't offer a design for life. But then they don't have to.'

New Musical Express hit the average at three stars, scribe Stuart Bailie suggesting *The Man Who* was 'over-loaded with ballads. Torch songs, slow blues, Gauloises-sucking chansons, requiems, every shade of indigo. Which is all right if you're Billie Holiday or Frank Sinatra. But if you're a bunch of rock blokes from Glasgow, the result isn't necessarily tremendous. Travis will be the best,' he concluded, 'when they stop trying to make sad, classic records.'

Released in late May 1999, Travis's second album nudged its way into the UK chart on 5 June at No. 5, four positions superior to its predecessor. This was the summer of the new *Star Wars*, and the music scene was somewhat sterile. Top spot was monopolised by Abba, the now non-existent Scandinavians racking up their 225th chart week with *Abba Gold*. Another long-server, Shania Twain's year-old *Come On Over*, stood at No. 3. It was a disappointingly backward-looking market for bands like Cast (whose *Magic Hour* slid from 6 to 26 in emulation of *Good Feeling* a year and a half earlier) while Suede's *Head Music* had fallen from 1 to 7 to 21 to 27 in a month. The only credible band with staying power seemed to be Stereophonics, who celebrated three months of *Performance And Cocktails* selling well by holding steady one place above Travis's new entry.

'This time we've recorded it over six months in six different studios, using more instrumentation, and it's turned into this weirdly cohesive piece of work.'

If the Glaswegians hoped next week's chart would indicate a leap to the summit, then Boyzone's *By Request* disappointed them, pushing the whole Top 5 down a place. Even then, though, the lads managed to outsell Shed Seven's portentously/pretentiously-titled *Going For Gold – The Greatest Hits*. From these lofty heights, however, it would prove a steady slide from 13 to 19 where, in its fifth week of release (3 July), it would be certified gold (100,000 copies sold). This seemed to give the album renewed heart, as it then proceeded to move up one place in two successive weeks! All was going well for the album – even the band themselves were surprised at its momentum.

'The last album was recorded in four days and became this supposedly schizophrenic record,' Dougie stated. 'This time we've recorded it over six months in six different studios, using more instrumentation, and it's turned into this weirdly cohesive piece of work.'

'On a scale of one to ten it was a six.'

Even if you factored the transatlantic air fares into the equation, it seemed likely that, with its many months of recording and two producers' wages to pay, *The Man Who* would have been considerably more expensive than the four-day wonder that was *Good Feeling*. Label boss Macdonald wasn't discussing figures regarding the new release, only to hint that 'on a scale of one to ten it was a six.' That, though, was 'still a fraction of the cost of a lot of major records.' Even so, he admitted that Independiente wasn't exactly 'rolling in cash, so every album's make or break.' This one had made, and would continue to make, friends and money in equal proportions.

The first single from the new album would be 'Writing To Reach You', which made its appearance in the second week of March. An ingenious plan was hatched to promote it that camouflaged the fact that the band had yet to finish studio business. The 20,000 or so people who'd responded to the *Good Feeling* insert card found the lyrics coming through their door in the form of a postcard 'hand-written' by Fran – what could be more appropriate?

Those lucky enough to have access to the Internet could do more than just wait for the single to hit the shops. Guided by the band's website address, they could log on and mail the band electronically. The next step was to put a web-cam in the rehearsal room and show the band limbering up for the forthcoming tour – apparently a first for any band, though it's a tactic many have copied since. Such space-age marketing had the desired effect, and the single flew into the chart at a band best of No. 14. Momentum was gathering.

The bonus songs available with the A-side were a pair of long-time concert favourites, 'Green Behind The Ears' and 'Only Molly Knows' (on CD1), plus another live staple 'Yeah, Yeah, Yeah, Yeah' and 'High As A Kite' (CD2). *New Musical Express*, the hatchet-men back at King's College in February, had a change of heart and gave the single an unequivocal thumbs-up. 'Superb stuff from Travis here, even if it is basically some superb stuff you might have heard a few times before, only then it was by Oasis and called 'Wonderwall.' Nevertheless, this pulls off a remarkable feat of anthemic schmaltziness without even curdling to cheese.' *Select* likewise took up the obvious comparison, but found in Travis's favour.

The video for the album's first single was clearly very important – and though its meaning may be impenetrable, who can forget Fran coming under attack form all manner of things from a German Messerschmitt to a little girl with a bow and arrow? Once seen, never forgotten... and when the finished result was put onto the official Travis website, work of mouth ensured 1800 hits a week. Interestingly, the special effects company used was the one that worked on *Saving Private Ryan* – a fact that went down predictably well with film-buff Healy, who saw Travis as 'a group of people that you have a common bond with; in our case, I don't know... going to the pictures or something. We've got this thing about proper bands. Proper bands are bands that didn't want to be in a band but just stumbled together and just fell into it.'

Dougie agreed, citing U2 or REM as bands with a similar 'shared history of shared experiences that makes them that much stronger.' Right now, Travis were moving from strength to strength.

CHAPTER EIGHT

SINGIN' IN THE RAIN

'Writing To Reach You' had served notice of the arrival of a new, mellow Travis – and when Radio 1's Steve Lamacq interviewed the band in February 1999 for his *Evening Session* programme it was clear something was in the air. 'It sounded great on the radio,' admitted its author.

But even more compelling a reason for this single to succeed than its first evening exposure was the patronage of Radio 1 breakfast-time queen Zoe Ball, who frankly grabbed the song and played it relentlessly. As her 'Record Of the Week', it cropped up every morning, sometimes twice! Fatboy Slim (her future husband) had come in at No. 1 with 'Praise You' after enjoying similar patronage, while the previously chart-shy Terrorvision had entered just one place lower with 'Tequila'.

She'd fallen in love with Travis, she explained, after listening to the single non-stop one weekend in her car. 'It's a beautiful record –

everyone goes all thoughtful when they hear it. I'm really, really looking forward to their album... ' By the time 'Driftwood' was released in May, she'd have just a week to wait...

Fran's *Cheers* and Fairy Liquid-inspired ode followed the by-now established pattern of entering the chart at its peak – fans having been galvanised by Independiente's efficient communications systems. On its side was a place on Radio 1's coveted A-list, ensuring it would be heard throughout the nation in a way its writer had long dreamed of. The unlikely help of Lamacq and Zoe had, it seemed, worked the oracle.

'You can leave here by walking down the stairs or I can drag you out by your balls.'

The video for 'Driftwood' was memorable in that it took Travis back to their schooldays – well, it might have done had any of them gone to a girls' school! The girls concerned were scripted to run for cover as the rain starts, leaving Travis and the teachers to get well and truly drenched. The distinctive album packaging would be reflected in all the videos for the singles – and that was far from a coincidence, as the directors involved were all issued with the covers as a template. The result, as Independiente marketing manager Anthony McGee pointed out, is instant recognition. 'Now you know if a poster or frame of a video is Travis even before you see any type.'

Fran was delighted that this particular song came by a lot more airplay than any Travis single to date. 'Radio is the advert space,' he explained, 'the trailer of one song for the whole album.' As for editing songs down to get them the longed-for airplay, 'I'm happy so long as I do the chopping...'

Beating 'Writing To Reach You's performance by a single place to establish itself as the most successful Travis single so far, 'Driftwood' might well have done better still had there not been no fewer than six new entries occupying the dozen places above it – including Manchester United's FA Cup anthem 'Be My Baby' (a cover of the 1960s girl group classic from Phil Spector's beehived Ronettes).

Travis had always enjoyed a friendly relationship with Radio 1, and this was cemented further on 27 May at the Garage on Glasgow's Sauchiehall Street when they played a gig that was broadcast to the nation. Introduced by Steve Lamacq, they stormed through a set that gave Fran cause to pause for thought: three days after the album's release the crowd all knew the words. 'Its weird... '

The night had an embarrassing moment in store for Dougie, who 'got thrown out by a bouncer who thought I was barred.' Fran: 'The bouncer said "You can leave here by walking down the stairs or I can drag you out by your balls".' Dougie: 'I walked.' The following night, he and Fran played a mini-acoustic set at the Internet Link cafe down the road which was broadcast over the world wide web via travisonline.com.

As befitting a group whose members had known the indignity of day jobs, they'd recently showed their compassionate side by playing a low-pay benefit at Newcastle's Telewest Arena on 10 April. Sandwiched between the Divine Comedy and Space on the one hand and Ash on the other, Fran and company got the crowed clapping along gamely to 'All I Want To Do Is Rock', the line about working round the clock suddenly taking on a new, ironic meaning. It was a far cry from Red Wedge, Paul Weller and Billy Bragg's 1980s group of Labour-voting musicians, but a rare example of Travis going political for a cause close to their hearts. Ticket prices, incidentally, were pegged at the under-22 minimum hourly wage rate: £3.

Meanwhile, a Travis mini-tour took in Cambridge, Norwich, Wolverhampton, Edinburgh, Manchester, Sheffield, Exeter and London's Astoria, a favourite venue of the band's which they played on 15 June. Tickets there were £9.50, while the other venues were a modest £8.50; commendably, the band weren't out to cash in on their popularity.

The last week of July saw the album back in the Top 10, for the first time higher than Stereophonics, while the first week of August found it at No. 6, its best showing since the heady week of release. What next? A one-place rise is the answer, and then, suddenly, it was bidding to knock Boyzone off their perch. Only the Chemical Brothers and Jamiroquai had managed that in the past three months, the Irish lads bouncing back each time to reclaim their crown. How would they deal with the Celtic challenge?

'We weren't just an "also on this stage... ", it was people coming to check us out.'

By now, strong word of mouth had starting shifting copies of *The Man Who* in vast numbers. On 28 August came the knockout punch. The thirteenth week in the chart was unlucky for no one except Boyzone as Travis hit the top ('Taking Boyzone from behind... messy!' as Fran put it.) To add simultaneous reason for celebration, it was certified as a platinum-seller with 300,000 sales in the UK alone. Another week in pole position awaited them.

It may not exactly have been seasonal in its subject-matter, but 'Why Does It Always Rain On Me?' would prove one of the summer hits of 1999. Each of the CD formats would include a track from the latest album recorded live at the Link Cafe – 'Driftwood' and 'Slide Show' respectively – while bonus tracks included the unluckily excluded live fave 'Village Man' and a cover of Joni Mitchell's 'The Urge for Going'.

The festival season always means work for a band like Travis -

and 1999 was certainly going to be no different. With V99 at two venues, Glastonbury and of course T In The Park in their native Scotland kicking things off in mid-July, the calendar was beginning to look pretty full. It was Kelly Jones of Stereophonics, another 'festival-friendly' band, who ventured the opinion that these events were good for 'stealing other people's fans…' but unlike previous years, Travis were now crowd-pullers in their own right. 'The festivals this year were cool,' Fran would later recall. 'People were actually coming to see us for the first time. We weren't just an "also on this stage… ", it was people coming to check us out.'

At Scotland's own July jolly-up, T In The Park at Kinross, near Perth, a rabid home crowd were particularly anxious to acclaim their local heroes. Dougie, who admitted he'd only been to one festival as a punter, was a particular fan of the phenomenon. 'Festivals are brilliant fun because it's not really about the band, it's about the people, so the music's a backdrop. You catch up with other bands who you've met up with over the year.'

Unfortunately, a series of events meant that T In The Park – organised by the owner of Glasgow's beloved King Tut's Wah-Wah Hut – nearly became the exception that proved the rule. Technical hitches enhanced the pre-gig nerves of the band. Andy was worried the crowd would 'go mental and riot'; people were already being pulled out from under the sides of the tent where they were attempting to avoid fire regulations and add themselves to the crowd inside.

When the group eventually made it to the stage, a security guard wouldn't let them on, believing they were early for the next slot. Thankfully, Travis's manager persuaded him otherwise, calming a potential riot in the process. At 7.15, 45 minutes after the appointed time, Travis, kilt-clad to a man in deference to their home country, finally hit the stage.

That wasn't the only controversy to be had, either: this was the festival that would go down as the Manics Toilet Tantrum where, as singer-songwriter Billy Bragg revealed, the Welsh trio, who liked to think of themselves as men of the people, had allegedly installed their own Portaloo and hung a 'hands-off' notice on the door!

Travis's appearance, though third on the bill, raised the roof – if tents *have* a roof, that is. And Fran's actions in turning his back to the audience and lifting his 'skirts' to reveal blue and white 'Scottish flag' underpants basically meant they were home and dry without having to play a single note! Fran, who recalled his last visit to T In The Park had been five years earlier to see Oasis, called it 'an

'I'd suddenly acquired this weird double-barrelled surname, like "Huey-from-Fun-Loving Criminals"!'

incredible feeling.' And just as that had been the moment Oasis moved from being a sizeable cult to the nation's favourite rock 'n' roll band, so he could feel Travis on the cusp of a similarly momentous event.

The set list included a new song, 'Coming Around', which was only omitted from the second album at the very last minute: so close was it to inclusion that certain foreign copies exist with the song listed on the sleeve (though not on the disc). It's a song certain reviewers have likened to legendary early-1970s American outfit Big Star, though Fran has possibly delved even further back to the Byrds. Live, it required another guitar part to be contributed live by guitar tech Nick... a step-up for a lad whose previous contribution to the entertainment on the band bus had been to take £5 dares for eating tubes of toothpaste and sticking ice cubes down his Y-fronts!

Fran remembers Glastonbury, with its heavy BBC radio and TV coverage, as being a real turning point in bringing the band into the nation's living rooms and transforming Travis into a household name. When he got home and turned on the box, 'everyone in the studio was going "Fran from Travis this" and "Fran from Travis that". I'd suddenly acquired this weird double-barrelled surname, like "Huey-from-Fun-Loving Criminals"!'

The new album's hidden track, 'Blue Flashing Light', kicked off

a 15-song set performed on Glastonbury's Other Stage with energy a-plenty. An ebullient Fran, surfing on the waves of goodwill from the crowd, had even dispensed some public service information between songs: 'Anyone got chronic sunburn? (Cheers) Don't use butter! (Groans)' But in a pre-gig Radio 1 interview, he'd cast doubt on the likelihood of the good weather lasting. 'I bet you any money it's going to rain – I've got a feeling about it.'

Sure enough, the heavens opened as the final chord of 'Why Does It Always Rain On Me?' died away. Just as the 'no rain' chant had become part of rock folklore at the original Woodstock thirty years earlier, this would go down in Glasto history and help turn newly tabloid-friendly Travis into the media focus of the festival.

'It fell in a very heavy way, really big raindrops like a summer shower,' Fran recalled later. 'Refreshing but annoying at the same time. And there were all these people looking up and going "You *bastards...*"'

Musically, though, this was a real triumph. As *Melody Maker* reported, Travis played 'like conquering Napoleons, lacing 'Good Day To Die' with guitar noises so sleazy they must have found them on Gary Glitter's hard drive, and shaking the Tor with a devastating 'Turn'. Growing up early has never been so graceful.'

Just before the show, the band had stopped by *Select* magazine's signing tent to press the flesh, practice their autographs and, touchingly, be presented with gifts as disparate as friendship bracelets and Frisbees. They weren't, they explained, camping this year, but would be splitting afterwards for a well-deserved break – Fran to an island (wisely unnamed) off the west coast of Scotland and Dougie off to Los Angeles for a week with his girlfriend. Neil, meanwhile, was the group's married man, though pipe and slippers were not (yet) in evidence!

There were happy echoes of the Oasis tour's opening nights at V99 in August, when Fran was able to announce from the stage to the 20,000-plus multitude that they had hit the top of the charts. 'There was no animosity, just a cheer of goodwill and thousands of happy people,' recalls Neil from behind the kit. Though Fran moaned that 'We always said we'd go the whole hog if we ever had a No. 1,' the band made do with warm beer in plastic cups to toast their success.

There'd been yet another daft run-in with festival security that reminded Travis that, though they might collectively be responsible the nation's No. 1 album, individually they were still far from household names... or more to the point faces. As Fran exited the stage after the band's main set, the legendary James Brown was arriving backstage in preparation for his. Security guards, seeing the Travis frontman heading their way in a rush of post-gig adrenaline, took him as someone who was about to attack said soul superstar and rugby-tackled him en masse.

Fortunately the promoter smoothed things over, there were no broken bones and Fran could see the funny side of things. But the humour wasn't over; as he headed back on stage to play the encore, a fan walked past him into full view of the mystified audience, dropped his trousers and, in an amazed Fran's words, 'blew us off the stage… literally!'

Looking at Travis's itinerary for August, it was amazing they had time to break wind. Earlier that month, they'd been double-booked by the Beeb to appear on the Radio 1 Roadshow in Newquay on the morning of the 12th before flying back to London for a *Top Of The Pops* session. They'd already played two more roadshows for the Beeb that summer, on 27 July, and two acoustic tracks with Mark Radcliffe and the Boy Lard at Whitby Bay on 6 August; in neither case were boys playing their armpits encountered…

Ironically given *Top Of The Pops*' reputation, the miming came in the morning rather than the afternoon, so all they had to pack was their instruments. Flying the flag for rock along with Liverpool scallies Cast, they rubbed shoulders with Enrique Iglesias, son of Latin god Julio, and boy band BBMak before hightailing it to the waiting executive aircraft, hired at a cool £800 per hour.

This time, they were sharing bar space with Barbara Windsor and Ross Kemp. But while Babs clearly dressed down for her role as Queen Vic landlady Peggy Mitchell, Fran was still resplendent in the denims and T-shirt he'd worn all day for each performance. 'We went to Albert Square, me and my girlfriend,' Fran revealed, and took pictures of ourselves "doing a Grant" and crying…

'I remembered *Top Of The Pops* from a child,' he continued enthusiastically, 'things from the 1980s like Dexys Midnight Runners, Nik Kershaw, Paul Young and Culture Club. You see the crowds. I loved it - I was talking to someone yesterday who didn't like *TOTP* when they went in because it was all strip-lighting, very bare and sterile . But I had a great time.'

For so many people, *The Man Who* was effectively Travis's first album – they'd never caught a glimpse of *Good Feeling* as it shot into and slid out of the charts with amazing rapidity two years earlier. Mindful of this, the band agreed to Independiente withdrawing and re-packaging their debut, replacing the original's childish design with something more considered – a serious group shot of the quartet against a black background. It was re-issued on 29 November and, by the end of 1999, had sold in excess of 50,000 copies in both versions – not bad.

They recalled the time when opening for Oasis when fans who'd just cottoned onto the Mancunians through *(What's The Story) Morning Glory* had failed to recognise first album songs like 'Live Forever'. 'I want that to happen with us,' Fran had said then, adding 'I can't wait for people to hear our third album and think it's our debut, like REM's *Out Of Time*.

No one could really understand why *The Man Who* had taken off in the way it did. 'You know how some albums say something about you? But with this album,' he concluded, 'it's not like you're buying into anything. It's not like a badge. You put it on your stereo, listen to it and that's it. I suppose it's like buying a wooden chair that serves a purpose. You just sit on it.'

It was a transformation that critics could liken to Dire Straits, whose *Brothers In Arms* became the *de rigueur* compact disc of the 1980s... yet ended up in a backlash of 'bland' accusations. But this was the break-through Fran Healy had long sought. Back in 1997, he'd belittled the trend-setting rock press, saying 'Most people read *Hello*, not *New Musical Express* and that's where I'm coming from. I'm interested in the 95 per cent not the five per cent.' It was as well he took a Kipling-esque stance to praise and criticism. Since then, he and his band had ridden the flak – most notably that damning live review in the self-same *New Musical Express* – and made it to the *Hello* readership. It wasn't so much selling out as the common touch. As Neil put it, 'At the moment Travis aren't *for* the people, they're *with* the people.'

The gap between the festivals and Travis's long-awaited British tour was filled with ventures to foreign fields. First stop was Japan, where long-suffering Dougie first contracted tonsillitis, then came out in spots as a reaction to the pills he was told to take! He played on regardless, fulfilling the band's four dates at Osaka, Nagoya (twice) and Tokyo – as the whole band did in Rome when their gig was broadcast live on national radio. Next stop Scandinavia, where they enjoyed nights on the town with fellow Scot Bobby Gillespie from Primal Scream and his pal, ex-Stone Rose Mani Mountfield.

Travis had last played Barrowlands with Catatonia and Idlewild

'Scotland fans were singing "Happy" – now that's priceless to me, way better than a No. 1 or a Brit award.'

way back in 1997. So there could be no better place to start their second major headlining tour of the UK – the first as a chart-topping act. And, though the night of 5 October coincided with a football international at Hampden Park, there was not a spare square foot in the house – nor any lack of terrace fervour to be found in an audience that simply would not let them go. American support band Remy Zero had appeared with Travis on the bill at T In The Park, and opened a show for which the queues had been building since 3pm, scalped tickets 'retailing' at a cool £60. But the crowd were there to see the main attraction, the hometown heroes who took the stage to the suitably appropriate strains of 'On The Street Where You Live' and kicked off proceedings with an equally familiar 'All I Want To Do is Rock'. There was a touch of self-indulgence as childhood photos were projected onto the backdrop during 'Slide Show', but that could be forgiven – these guys were revelling in some totally deserved home-town adulation. As they prepared to sign off for the night, twenty songs lighter but with fans a good deal happier, Fran bade them all a fond farewell. 'We've had an amazing night. This is our last song and I'd like to dedicate it to you. It's important in life to be sad – but it's as important to be "Happy".' He later termed it 'the most fucking awesome gig we have ever done.'

Ironically, given Scotland's simultaneous Euro 2000 win against Bosnia (the audience kept Travis informed of the score by means of hand signals), Travis had at one point been asked to write a contender for the Scotland World Cup song – a job eventually given to Del Amitri, a band they've often been compared with. 'More importantly to me, though, is that when Scotland got into the World Cup the Scotland fans were singing "Happy" – now that's priceless to me, way better than a No. 1 or a Brit award.'

The tour wound on through Dundee and Aberdeen to cross the border at Newcastle. Next came Sheffield, Leeds, Hull, Leicester, Bristol, Cardiff, Reading, Nottingham, Liverpool and Manchester, with tales to be told at each venue en route – usually from the stage by Fran. For instance, before the Aberdeen gig the band had visited a school to spread the word about 'Drop The Debt', the Bono-sponsored campaign to free the Third World from its onerous and effectively unpayable obligations to the West. As the band said their goodbyes and set about leaving on the tour bus, three intrepid and well prepared schoolboys dropped their trousers to reveal the letters TR, AV and IS on each of their backsides!

In many of the venues (the Universities, especially) there was a realisation that this would be the last time Travis fans would see them in a venue this small and compact. The prices being demanded by the touts outside unfortunately reflected that too. Yet for all those who couldn't get in, but had access to the Internet, there was at least the compensation of a regularly undated Tour Diary from the band, augmented by pictures from the gigs thanks to the digital camera revolution.

For the first time since 1996, their sound was augmented by keyboards, one Jeremy Proctor – who 12 months earlier had been working at a fish merchant's in Morecambe, Lancashire – adding his talents to the mix; a master of the scales, perhaps? One reporter grabbed a chat with Jeremy after the show at Leeds Town and Country, and his comments betrayed the huge weight of expectation Travis now carried with them in live performance, not just from their audience but themselves. 'I really enjoyed tonight's show and I am surprised to learn that the others are not sure we played that well. I think that this self-criticism, though, is probably why these four have made Travis the band it is...'

The tour continued to Lancaster, then headed ever southwards through Oxford, Birmingham, Portsmouth and Folkestone before ending in the capital at Shepherd's Bush Empire on the last day of October. The kilts made another reappearance to celebrate, while the following day would see Travis in the *Later* studios for a reunion with Jools Holland.

From its August high point until the third week of November, *The Man Who* had been a fixture in the Top 5, wilting only under the triple threat of Queen, Five and Steps. Even then, it bounced back and, unbelievably, on 15 January 2000 deposed Shania Twain to regain the No. 1 slot once more, becoming the first new home-grown album of the new millennium in the process. There must have been a lot of people who woke up on Christmas morning to find the Travis album in their stocking, because during the course of December sales grew from three times platinum (900,000 sold) to five times.

'Turn' had become the fourth single from the album in early November, and coming from a Top 5 album was sure of attention. It must have been a thrill for Fran to find that *Melody Maker's* guest reviewer the week before release was none other than Jarvis Cocker of Pulp, no mean wordsmith himself and an ex-art scholar to boot. He was obviously acquainted with the band's work, though he thought the song 'slightly maudlin. When you hear their songs,' he continued, warming to his theme, 'you find them quite dull, but they do often become quite catchy the more you hear them.'

The Sheffield singer's three out of five rating happily

wasn't shared by an ever-increasing army of Travis fans out there in singles-land, who accorded the band their highest chart placing yet. At No. 8, it had climbed two rungs higher than 'Why Does It Always Rain On Me?', and that in the traditionally tough Christmas marketplace inhabited this year by everyone but the Spice Girls. Those who'd bought the album (and who hadn't, by now?) were rewarded as usual by bonus tracks spread across the two formats. The first compact disc offered 'River' the new 'Days Of Our Lives' and the 'Turn' video in CD-ROM form for computer-literates, while the second disc accompanied the lead song's radio edit with another new song, 'We Are Monkeys', and, immortalised for the first and only occasion, 'Baby One More Time'.

Recorded by 17-year-old former Disney starlet Britney Spears, 'Baby… ' was the single of 1999 just as certainly as Travis had scooped the album honours; Noel Gallagher, no less, would term her debut single his pick of the year. Britney, who'd started the year a total unknown in Britain, was in all other respects not of their universe. Her first act on reaching the age of majority was rumoured to have been augmenting her figure by artificial means (though she never confirmed this officially).

It all seemed highly unlikely that the repertoires of Britney Spears and Travis would ever overlap in the slightest detail – until, that was, Fran picked up on the lyric that lay underneath the sugar coating. 'There's a real sinister undercurrent,' he explained, 'and it's a well put-together song. I learned it as a joke, but then I realised what a brilliant song it was. I don't think I could write a song this perfect.' Having 'learned it for a laugh,' he was soon heard to implore the nation to 'Hit me one more time' after waxing it for the Mark and Lard afternoon show. It then found its way into the stage act, being typically introduced thus: 'By popular demand, one of the greatest songs ever – even if we didn't write it.'

The video for 'Turn' (director of photography, Andrezcj Sekula, did *Reservoir Dogs*) was impressive stuff, involving Fran in having to do 300 press-ups, and was shortlisted for March 2000's MTV Video

awards. Emma Bunton, alias Baby Spice, said she found the effect 'upsetting', while presenter Richard Blackwood highlighted the fact that the clip was 'like a home video, simple but real – he's got a realness about him.'

Meanwhile, 11 November found the band back in their home city of Glasgow where they'd opened their tour so successfully five weeks earlier. But this wasn't to be a return visit to the beloved 'Barras', but a surprise open-air 'thank you' concert on a specially erected stage outside the Royal Concert Hall. November was hardly the month to go camping out, but a queue numbering some hundreds of intrepid Travis-ites formed early in the morning outside the Virgin Megastore at the top of Buchanan Street. Their aim was to obtain a security wristband which would give them access to the concert the following night; as the *Evening Times* reported, St. Andrew Ambulance volunteers were on hand to ensure they survived to claim their tickets, handing out woollen blankets and special tinfoil cloaks to those who had come less than adequately prepared as the temperature dropped to below zero.

The gig itself was as hot as the night had been cold. Taking the stage to an audience-participation version of 'Wonderwall', Fran, Dougie, Andy and Neil lashed into 'All I Want To Do Is Rock', Fran's vocals showing no sign of raggedness despite the wear and tear of the tour. Unfortunately, it later emerged that thieves had stolen two guitars from backstage and were seen trying to sell them in a local pub. Happily both were later recovered...

The year-end polls for 1999 were nothing less than a Travis-fest. And it was in *Melody Maker*, who'd given them their first front cover back in December 1997, where their presence was felt most deeply. 'Best Album', 'Best Single' ('... Rain... '), 'Best New Band', 'Haircut of the Year' (Fran, obviously)... it was a total victory. Fran was understandably delighted. He did, however, temper pride with a winning modesty. When quizzed about edging the 'Best Album' honour over Stereophonics' *Performance And Cocktails* he had this to say: 'All the kids care about is to get off on one, dance and smile to some good music. In ten years' time, people will look back at both records and go "They are great albums." No-one will remember which of them was ‚Album of the Year, and even if they do it really won't matter.' To keep them down to earth, Andy recalled a friend who worked in a Camden record store telling him about the guy who took back his copy of because he found it 'too depressing'!

'Every time we play that song, it rains... We played it at Glastonbury, it started raining. We were quite afraid, I thought we were going to get bottled off...'

On to the *Q* Awards, where a slightly older age group gave Travis their unqualified approval. The award, presented by Radio 1's Jo Whiley, was for 'Why Does It Always Rain On Me?', voted top single by *Q* readers and the station's listeners. The band were also nominated in the 'Best Album' and 'Best New Act, but beating Supergrass, Blur and company to the 'Best Single' award was a thrill. His favourite among the contenders (New Radicals and Lauryn Hill being the others) was female hip-hop trio TLC's 'No Scrubs'.

There was plenty of fun to be had, too, at the post-award shindig. New Order's Peter Hook presented them with his autograph, while Fran shook hands with Ian Dury, a long-time hero. He also palled up with Blur's Damon Albarn (sporting a suspiciously familiar hairstyle) and was photographed feeding Alex James with a string of grapes as the other three looked on amused.

The previous day had seen them make their second appearance on *Later*, the show that had launched them to fame. Having just played two songs on that occasion, it was their turn this time to be put under the spotlight as their affable host invited Fran and Dougie to share his piano stool. They revealed that as well as having 'supported everybody' since their last appearance, they'd also played the wedding of their music publisher, Charlie Pinder. ('I remember there was a big, red double-decker bus that took us from the wedding to the reception, said Dougie. 'I was wearing my Beatles suit.')

Three songs, all singles, were performed – 'Driftwood', Turn' and 'Why Does It Always Rain On Me?' with Dougie expounding on the self-fulfilling prophecy of the last-named. 'Every time we play that song, it rains. It was raining in Israel when Fran wrote it, it was raining in France when we recorded it. We played it at Glastonbury, it started raining. We were quite afraid, I thought we were going to get bottled off...'

This particular *Later* turned out to be as memorable as its predecessor, not least because Paul McCartney was spotted singing along to 'Turn'. Dougie kept his cool... but only just! Fran would go one better when he actually played with Sir Thumbs Aloft on TV show *The Millennium Tube* – an honour Mr Payne admitted made him very jealous indeed. 'I was at the back glowing green, muttering you *bastard*... ' (They'd have yet another chance to hobnob with Sir Paul in early 2000 at the Brats awards, sponsored by the *New Musical Express*, where Travis won 'Best Artist'; the ex-Beatle was being honoured for his lifetime achievement.)

The positioning of two pre-Christmas gigs at the Barrowlands meant Travis could, in Bob Dylan's immortal phrase, 'bring it all back home' to the citizens of their home city. Support act the Clint Boon Experience, headed by the former Inspiral Carpets organist, appreciated they were very much the spare parts at the wedding, and kept their set mercifully brief, punctuated as it was by cheer-inspiring statements that Travis were 'the hottest fucking band in Britain'.

Once Travis were on stage, things very nearly turned nasty when someone threw a pint of beer at the centre-stage microphone area, causing Fran to stop the show and have the house lights turned up. The miscreant was not apprehended, but happily the show continued after that justifiable flash of temper. The second show saw Travis take the stage at the unusually early hour of seven, this allowing the band, crew and venue staff the chance to join their family for the seasonal festivities.

It was already clear, though, that this would be the last home fans would see of Travis for a while. 'We just want to pull out for a bit,' Fran would explain, 'because we're bloody everywhere at the moment. It's ridiculous!' You suspect, though, he said it with a smile playing on his lips... and no wonder. Barrowlands box office had sold out of tickets within two hours of going on sale. And Travis had always believed in the showbusiness maxim that you should leave your audience wanting more…

A triple-headed package round Europe with Gay Dad and the Ben Folds Five gave Travis the chance to explore their new confidence. And though the package was nominally one of equals, a set lasting barely 40 minutes the result, from the crowd reaction there was little doubt who the stars of the show were. It was ironic, really; in the midsummer when Travis-mania first burst, Fran had been positively looking forward to playing places they had yet to become known. 'We're starting completely from scratch,' he'd said of playing in Europe. 'I'm obsessed with keeping my feet on the ground, and I think that will help us do that. It'll be like going back three years…'

There was no doubt about it, 1999 had been one hell of a year for Travis. They'd entered it as cult heroes and ended it, as the cover of *Q* magazine had emblazoned in letters two inches high, 'Britain's Favourite Band!' It was only right that the year should end with a bang, and that's exactly what it had done.

THE GLASGOW
SCHOOL
OF ART
167

CHAPTER NINE

COMING AROUND AGAIN

Having sold 1.45 million albums in 1999, making them the fifth biggest sellers in the UK behind Shania Twain, Boyzone, Corrs and Steps, level with Stereophonics, and unbelievably ahead of Robbie Williams, George Michael and Celine Dion, Travis had earned the right to take the first month of the new millennium off before considering their next move (Neil spent his free time mountain-biking in Scotland).

After taking to America, a third album was uppermost on the agenda, and was likely to be recorded in the summer in Los Angeles, away from the pressure of the home-based media. And Fran was already certain it was going to be 'one of the most optimistic records ever made.' As well as the now-familiar 'Coming Around', it was likely to feature another song called 'Afterglow'... though after previous last-minute chopping and changing, no one was likely to bet on it just yet.

The songs would once again be Fran's, though Dougie and Andy were both keen to chip in compositions of their own. And that was something Fran positively welcomed. He'd rationalised the fact that, as the band's sole songwriter, he'd be paid more than the others by the fact that creating songs was 'something I fucking hate', but admitted he'd be happier in a situation not unlike the latter-day Beatles, where competition between writers drove them to ever higher pinnacles for artistic achievement. 'They'd better be fucking good songs, though,' he jokingly warned his colleagues.

'The better the song the better you, as a guitarist, will sound – and he makes the rest of us sound better.'

It seemed unlikely, though, that Fran would be usurped as creator-in-chief and mouthpiece of the band. And contrary to what had been hinted elsewhere, Andy seemed remarkably modest in his ambitions when quizzed by *Q* magazine. It wasn't his aim to write a Travis song, he explained. 'I'm quite happy to be a good guitarist. People get overly ambitious. The important thing is to remember why you're doing it and what you're good at.' He admired Fran as a songwriter because 'the better the song the better you, as a guitarist, will sound – and he makes the rest of us sound better.'

The vocal spotlight looked more likely to be shared around more evenly in future: indeed, Dougie had for some while been singing the second verse of 'Turn' live. 'Frannie ran out of breath in practice one time and said "Dougie, you sing it."' The new single will contain the track 'Just The Faces Change', written and sung by Dougie.

As for what the coming years would hold, well, who could say? It could hardly be as cataclysmic as the final year of the old millennium... but then again, a US No. 1 would do the trick quite nicely! Travis's first US tour had been in November 1997, just as *Good Feeling* was unleashed upon the largely uncomprehending Yanks. As a stop-gap before their next full-scale effort, the quartet played selected Stateside dates in early 2000.

Though Fran had previously pooh-poohed the importance of breaking in the States, he was singing a slightly different tune when interviewed prior to the Brit Awards. 'America is important to us,' he said, 'and we will just keep going back there and banging away until we make it. Some bands think they can go there and break it like that, but we know it's going to take hard work. But we do want to sell records all over the world.'

For these dates, Fran had come to LA a couple of weeks before the others to visit friends. He was enjoying the anonymity – until he took a walk along Sunset Strip and saw a British magazine on a news-stand with his picture on the front. 'It was like a double take because you don't expect, it, you're in a totally different country.' If all went well it was the kind of surprise he'd better get used to...

One of these gigs was at Los Angeles' famed Troubadour Club, handily situated on Santa Monica Boulevard, which was the venue where Elton John made such a big early-1970s splash from which the Americans never quite recovered! It's said there were more stars in the audience that night than on-stage – and certainly it remains the place to get yourself noticed. And just to prove Travis could also draw more then just common-or-garden punters, Stereophonics singer Kelly Jones and fellow Welshman Rhys (*Twin Town, Notting Hill*) Ifans were there to lend their support.

Unfortunately, the Troubadour gig got off to a shaky start... primarily because of the previously mentioned star guests in the crowd. Kelly had taken it upon himself to leap up on stage totally unannounced, embrace Travis's singer and announce 'Fran Healy, this is your life', and exit stage left, closely followed by his compatriot

Ifans – and Fran, who thought the film star was the 'Phonics' bass player Richard Jones(!), admitted he was totally thrown. 'It was nice to see him (Kelly), though.'

It was early February, with still over two months from US release, so this was really just a warm-up for the main event, with five shows in the States and one north of the border in Canada. The gig before the Troubadour had been at an appropriately named San Francisco club called the Bottom of the Hill. Little wonder Fran reckoned that, despite their previous foray, they were basically starting from scratch again. Not that he saw breaking the States as the be all and end all of his existence.

People here say we're like a breath of fresh air... a lot of them can't stand Korn and Blink 182, so I guess we're quite refreshing.'

'America's just the next place after Britain and Europe. Put us anywhere and we'll do what we're doing. Whether people get it or don't get it is up to the climate of the time. People here say we're like a breath of fresh air... a lot of them can't stand Korn and Blink 182, so I guess we're quite refreshing.'

Certainly, the home-grown likes of the bands he named, plus Limp Bizkit and Kid Rock, plus the pop sirens of the Spears/Aguilera school (however great their songs) left plenty of vacant middle ground to be occupied. Travis were simply planting their flag.

A week later, they'd crossed the continent to New York, where the Bowery Ballroom played host to them – sold out at a reasonable $12 (£9 a ticket). It was clearly a buzz for Travis to be playing the clubs again: 'I don't think any band's a stadium band,' said Fran. And though there's usually a buzz of conversation at such venues, the punters having come along for a drink and a chat as much as the show, you could hear a pin drop during the quiet bits... of which there are more than a few in a Travis show.

Fran loved the Bowery in particular. 'It's an amazing venue, like a miniature theatre or an old-fashioned dance hall. All the gigs were three quarters industry people and one quarter people who were into the band and wanted to check us out. Even given that fact, we got a warm reception.'

One of those 'industry people' was a correspondent from *Billboard* magazine, the major US trade paper, who was bowled over by what he saw and heard. The band's inspiring, insistently melodic folk-rock sound had, he believed, gone a long way in opening new ears to the so-called 'Travis Phenomenon.' 'There was no shortage of exuberant audience members familiar with the band's back catalogue, from which older tracks such as 'All I Want To Do Is Rock' and 'Happy' were extracted. Travis even unveiled a new (sic) song, 'Coming Around,' which featured a lucky friend (sic... er, Nick!) of the band on guitar.'

However successful they proved as a live act, Travis were certainly facing an uphill struggle in the States to get airplay. 'If it doesn't rock it don't get on' is the motto. And while San Francisco, New York, and Los Angeles have record stores that stock import sounds and radio stations that play them, the citizens of Anytown, Illinois are unlikely to have such free and unfettered access to new music. It's a strange scenario where songs are released to radio sometimes without ever physically being pressed up as singles the public can buy.

The hope, Fran explained, was that one song would capture public imagination and find its own wings. 'Once the song is out there it doesn't actually need a band – it'll go off and do its little thing.' An unlikely ally was found in MTV, the cable music television channel, which invited Travis to play host to a *120 Minutes* 'alternative rock' programme to be screened in late February. Meanwhile they hoped to take advantage of the fact that the producer of the *Total Request Live* programme, one Deborah Savo, was a fan. It would even be worth playing 'Baby One More Time' if only to get a reaction.

Certainly, its appearance as the US mini-tour encore, with Fran and Dougie strumming for all they're worth, brought the house down. According to *Melody Maker*, they were 'commenting on the sad state of American pop culture while simultaneously exalting it.'

They'd be back in April to plug the album, released that month on the Epic label, but not alone: the announcement came as they were out there that Travis would be touring as the opening act for Oasis. Fran insisted he had no expectations of making it big. But the suspicion voiced by the *Melody Maker* reporter sent out to follow their every move in the US remained: could they just be 'too good for post-millennial America'?

The argument would be decided once and for all in the period between Wednesday 5 April 2000 when they kicked off in Seattle's Paramount Theatre. Unlike Travis, who'd fizzed with their first album and burned with their second, the Gallaghers had followed two triumphs with the comparative artistic disappointment that was *Be Here Now* – the album they'd been promoting the last time Travis had crossed their path. They'd also lost two band members, 'Bonehead' Arthurs and 'Guigsy' McGuigan, in the course of recording their fourth opus, *Standing On the Shoulder Of Giants*, and had much to prove. One thing was for sure: it would be much more of an even contest than the last time the bands had toured together.

Ironically, an interviewer in August 1999 had touted Andy for the vacant guitarist's post. He offered this answer – one that said much about Travis's unique fellow feeling. 'Oasis are a great band, but I'd prefer to stay with my mates. That's the whole shame about this thing (Oasis's split) is that they were all mates. It must be horrible for anyone (new) to go into that and not really know any of them... I'm sure it's a great job,' he concluded, 'but I'm happy where I am.'

Starting on the West Coast at the home of grunge (anyone recall the Kurt Cobain meets Marti Pellow references way back when?), the Oasis/Travis teaming would head south to Universal City, California, before travelling inland to Chicago and Detroit. Philly and Boston were to be followed by a swift trip over the border to Toronto before New York, Fairfax, Charlotte and finally Atlanta's Music Midtown Festival. It all added up to exactly a month on the road, taking in 18 cities.

Travis would warm up for this excursion with a seven-date mini European tour in late March, taking in Amsterdam, Paris, Offenbach, Hamburg, Berlin, Munich and Cologne. To speed them on their way, Radio 1 broadcast its own version of their story on 6 March at 11pm as part of Steve Lamacq's show. The documentary, entitled *Meeting the Beatles Is Easy*, was compiled and presented by Danny O'Connor; 'the most comprehensive ever made' about the band, it covered the events of the last three years with contributions from the quartet, management, producer Nigel Godrich and Noel Gallagher.

Three days before that, though, came the Brit Awards. With Stereophonics having cleaned up in 1999, Travis' were bidding to do likewise, having been nominated in the categories of 'Best Band', 'Best Album' and 'Best Single' (for 'Why Does It Always Rain On Me?').

Like Stereophonics, Travis were firmly flying the rock flag, since dance acts dominated the year's other nominations. Chemical Brothers topped the list with four nominations, while Basement Jaxx and Fatboy Slim earned three nods each. Travis were also scheduled to take part in the live line-up.

'We weren't putting another single out (from the album),' Fran explained, 'but it's a nice way to end things, what with 'Slide Show' being the last track on the album. There's not any reason really, other than making a wee film. It's like saying "See you in a while..."'

With its Byrds resonances, 'Coming Around' was not only guaranteed to be a British hit but could be the best chance of playing the Americans at their own game. Yet though it was scheduled for

UK release on 8 May – the first new A-side for just over a year – the debut Stateside single was still scheduled to be 'Why Does It Always Rain On Me?'. The US version of was scheduled to include three acoustic bonus tracks: 'Driftwood', 'Slide Show' (both from the Link Cafe sessions) and 'More Then Us' (recorded live by Italian radio).

The eighteenth annual Brit Awards ceremony at London's cavernous Earls Court was, as ever, attended by a mixture of music-biz top nobs, all dining on the company tab, and a bunch of youngsters from the Brits school, imported to mosh stage front after the television powers-that-be had complained of a lack of atmosphere.

Hosted by divinely fragrant TV personality Davina McCall, wrapped in a pink frock that could well have been one of Princess Di's cast-offs, the event was scripted down to the last cough and sneeze... apart, that was, from a stage-invading DJ accosting Rolling Stone Ron Wood and being told in no uncertain terms to go forth and multiply! Moving swiftly on, Ms McCall returned to her Teleprompter and read the following: 'These guys have been one of the great British success stories of recent years – so how come it always rains on Travis?'

Andy was resplendent on red trousers, Dougie beamed inanely as he plucked his Jazz bass, Fran wore a red pullie, acoustic guitar and kilt and Neil... was just being Neil. The Brit scholars immediately went into football-crowd mode, swaying with arms aloft – much like a Travis concert, actually – while the big-wigs rattled their cutlery in appreciation. 'There is something quite *glorious* about a man in a kilt,' grinned Davina in best scripted ad-lib style.

Ironically, the song Travis played was to miss out on the 'Best Single' honours, claimed for the second consecutive year by Robbie Williams. Back to darling Davina... 'It's one of the toughest categories to vote on,' she said, 'but the next people up here will be the 'Best Group'.' Presenting the trophy was the self-same rock icon Travis had last seen on his bike in New York – yes, Lou Reed! Could this be an omen?

Clips were shown of those seeking to emulate the Manics last year: Gomez, Blur, Stereophonics, Texas and Travis. 'And the winner is...Travis!' Fran led the group onto the stage holding his own video camera, neatly turning the tables on the film crew that had been lurking nearby – rather a give-away as to who'd won. Handshakes

all round with Mr Reed, then the acceptance speeches. Andy: 'They say that liquid paraffin is the best cure for constipation – but winning a Brit award has taken its place Thank you very much!' Fran: 'We want to thank our mums and dads for having us, our managers, Independiente, anyone else. We just want to say thank you, it means a lot to us.'

More gong-dishing ensued before Vinnie Jones, 'a man not to be messed with from Wimbledon to Hollywood' according to Davina's scriptwriter, took the stage. The white-suited ex-footballer started by assuring us that the fella who bothered his mate Ronnie Wood was 'completely fucking sorted' before attempting to sort out a winner from Basement Jaxx (*Remedy*), the Chemical Brothers (*Surrender*) Gomez (*Liquid Skin*) Stereophonics (*Performance And Cocktails*) and, of course, *The Man Who*. Seemingly operating scriptless, Vinnie opined that 'The only band that could beat the Stereophonics for the 'Best Album' award is... Travis!'

'Again, this is fantastic,' burbled Dougie, while Fran, as ever, had a more significant message. 'I'd like to dedicate this to people playing guitars on the ends of their beds, pianos or whatever you do. Keep doing it – these people will find you.' The bigwigs mumbled assent through their salmon vol au vents, and Travis's evening's work was complete. One song performed, two Brits won...!

The post-gig celebrations were enlivened by the opportunity to race motorised toilets go-kart style, as Prime Minister's wife Cherie Blair hobnobbed with the stars on the sidelines. Although Tom Jones kissed her on the cheek and Chris Evans cheekily patted her six-months-pregnant stomach, the *Mail On Sunday* reported 'she looked genuinely pleased to meet some of the younger stars including Scottish band Travis.' This accompanied a picture of Dougie, Fran and Cherie with matching postbox grins.

In an event bereft of true star quality, most critics believed the less showy acts like Travis – 'the genial Glaswegians whose uplifting tunes and thoughtful words beguiled a million record-buyers in 1999' – and 'Best British Female' Beth Orton had come out best. 'It was deeply unimpressive,' opined pop-star-turned-pundit Jonathan King, 'but I'm pleased for Travis.' The effect the exposure might have on sales was downplayed by HMV record-store boss Gennaro Castaldo. 'I can't see Travis or Robbie Williams selling any more, they've peaked,' he stated. But on a night like this, who the hell cared?

Home-based live shows for 2000 were still sketchy, particularly with the band so keen to write new material, but some slots were already pencilled in. Travis were the first confirmed bill-toppers for the inaugural Glastonbury of a new millennium. They'd headline the Saturday night, 24 June, with the Chemical Brothers and David Bowie the likely names for Friday and Sunday.

They were also likely to play T In The Park in July and the Virgin-sponsored V2000 Festival on 19 and 20 August at the twin venues of Chelmsford, Essex and Staffordshire – blanket coverage of the main events in similar fashion to the Manic Street Preachers in 1999.

The new single 'Coming Around' – actually an last-minute omission from *The Man Who* – previewed a new album for which there were already 'plenty of songs... it's probably going to be the most optimistic album you've ever heard.' This, if true, would contrast with the autumn/winter feel of *The Man Who*, but it seemed unlikely that album three wouldn't repeat the pattern of following on from its predecessor.

It would be interesting to see who'd be chosen to produce the next album proper. Nigel Godrich had gone straight from Travis to his other protegés Radiohead, who were having inordinate trouble coming up with a coherent fourth album (and they say it gets easier...) Travis had earlier recorded 'Flowers In The Window', the song Fran had composed on the piano in Mike Hedges' chateau, with Stephen Street of New Order/Pet Shop Boys fame, but all parties including Independiente had apparently not been totally happy with what had been produced.

Travis saw little of their home town these days. Glasgow was still the same, and the band professed not to miss it. 'We spent 23 years there,' Fran explains, ' so why would you miss something you're so familiar with?' One of their rare visits gave them pause for thought, however. Returning to the Horsehoe Bar for a drink at their early small venue/haunt - their first gig ever was there in front of 14 people - they saw that it hadn't actually changed much. Yet, despite all that had happened to them, it felt like only last week that they had played there. 'It was only when we left that we noticed there was one of those blue plaques screwed to the wall outside that read, "Travis, the band who recorded the No. 1 *The Man Who* album, played their first gig here." That was *mind-blowing...*'

Now resolutely London-based, Fran – announced as the year's third most successful songwriter in trade weekly *Music Week*, could enjoy some of the rewards. His abode was decorated by works of art from Super Furry Animals painter Pete Fowler and Glasgow School of Art graduate Michael Grant, and fully reflected his beliefs. 'Art, to me, boils down to something that has an effect on you, something that tells you about the world but also helps you to understand it.' As far as his personal life went, Fran had found a sympathetic partner in a German lady called Nora. As a fully qualified make-up artist, she can travel with the band and perform a vital backstage function.

'We may be a bit boring for some people. We just want to go out and give people a good night...'

Many songwriters in rock's history have totally lost the plot after finding personal happiness. Assuming Fran Healy managed this, would it all end? Back in 1997, he'd suggested that he would record five albums with Travis, then 'paint and have a family and be there while they're growing up.' And that made unarguable sense. After all, given his own one-parent upbringing (albeit with huge amounts of help from and contact with relatives) the last thing he wanted to be was an absentee rock 'n' roll father.

Ironic, then, that the April 2000-dated copy of *Q* magazine should include an interview with the dad Fran never knew. The story was headed 'The Dad Who... ' and was illustrated by a picture of Frank Healy watching a video of his son on his home television. It claimed he'd contacted *Q* in January 'with a heartfelt appeal for his son's forgiveness and a dramatic description of the events leading to his split with Fran's mother.'

This was, in effect, Healy Senior invoking his right to reply to an article two months earlier where Fran declared 'I don't have a dad'. Still Stafford-based, the former lorry driver, now retired, claimed 'I maintained that boy... never missed a payment,' and that he and his new family (son Ryan, daughters Nicky and Nathalie) had turned down offers of money from the tabloids for their story. I don't want to make money off my kids,' said Frank. 'All I want to do is talk to him.'

Whether or not he broke the silence with his father, it seemed certain that Fran Healy still had much to say to the world at large. 'The drummer from the Pretenders, Martin Chambers, he described the sound of our music as 'simplicity with weight,' and I thought he was quite accurate. He said we made him remember why he did this in the first place.

'With Travis, because of our attitude towards the whole thing – and we don't have much – we may be a bit boring for some people. But we're not so much interested in the big rock star thing. We just want to go out and give people a good night, a night they will remember without fucking putting on make-up or wiggling our bums too much. Because it's much more important than that...'

The last word, inevitably, is with Fran. Back in a 1997 interview with *Q* magazine, he expounded on what made Travis a great band, and he just about hit the nail on the head: 'Art is the background, music is the soundtrack. We work in this business so we think it's the most important fucking thing in the world. To most people, music is two decibels in the background. We're in the five per cent that thinks music is more important than it actually is...'

THE STORY OF TRAVIS

DISCOGRAPHY

SINGLES

As Glass Onion

'THE GLASS ONION EP'

Release date: 1993
Catalogue number: unknown
Highest chart position: n/a (limited edition)
Dream On; The Day Before; Free Soul;
Whenever She Comes Around

As Travis

ALL I WANT TO DO IS ROCK

Release date: November 1996
Catalogue number: Red Telephone Box PHONE 001
Highest chart position: n/a (limited edition of 750)
All I Want To Do Is Rock; The Line Is Fine; Funny Thing

U16 GIRLS

Release date: 1 April 1997
Catalogue number: ISOM 1MS
Highest chart position: 40
U16 Girls; Hazy Shades of Gold; Good Time Girls; Good Feeling

ALL I WANT TO DO IS ROCK

Release date: 16 June 1997
Catalogue number: ISOM 3MS/ISOM 3SMS
Highest chart position: 39
CD1: All I Want To Do Is Rock;
Blue on a Black Weekend; Combing My Hair
CD2: Track listing All I Want To Do Is Rock; "20"; 1922

TIED TO THE 90S

Release date: 4 August 1997
Catalogue number: ISOM 5MS/ISOM 5SMS
Highest chart position: 30
CD1: Tied to the 90s; City In The Rain;
Whenever She Comes Around; Standing On My Own
CD2: Tied to the 90s; Me Beside You

HAPPY

Release date: 13 October 1997
Catalogue number: ISOM 6MS/ISOM 6SMS
Highest chart position: 38
CD1: Happy; Unbelievers; Everyday Faces
CD2: Happy; When I'm Feeling Blue (Days of the Week);
Mother

MORE THAN US EP

Release date: 30 March 1998
Catalogue number: ISOM 11MS/ ISOM 11SMS
Highest chart position:16
CD1: More Than Us (with Anne Dudley);
Give Me Some Truth;
All I Want to Do Is Rock (with Noel Gallagher);
Funny Thing (with Tim Simenon)
CD2: More Than Us (with Anne Dudley);
Beautiful Bird (demo version); Reason (with Susie Hug);
More Than Us (acoustic)

WRITING TO REACH YOU
Release date: 8 March 1999
Catalogue number: ISOM 22MS/ISOM 22SMS
Highest chart position: 14
CD1: Writing to Reach You; Green Behind the Ears;
Only Molly Knows
CD2: Writing to Reach You; Yeah, Yeah, Yeah, Yeah;
High as a Kite

DRIFTWOOD
Release date: 17 May 1999
Catalogue number: ISOM 27MS/ ISOM 27SMS
Highest chart position: 13
CD1: Track listing Driftwood; Be My Baby; Where Is The Love
CD2: Track listing Driftwood;
Writing To Reach You (Deadly Avenger's Bayou Blues Mix);
W.T.R.Y. (Deadly Avenger's Instrumental Remix)

WHY DOES IT ALWAYS RAIN ON ME?
Release date: 2 August 1999
Catalogue number: ISOM 33MS/ISOM 33SMS
Highest chart position:10
CD1: Why Does It Always Rain on Me?;
Village Man; Driftwood (live at the Link Cafe)
CD2: Track listing Why Does It Always Rain on Me?;
The Urge for Going; Slide Show (live at the Link Cafe)

TURN
Release date: 8 November 1999
Highest chart position: 8
CD 1 (ISOM 39MS): Turn; River;
Days Of Our Lives; CD-rom Turn (video)
CD 2 (ISOM 39SMS): Turn (Radio Edit);
We Are Monkeys; Baby One More Time

COMING AROUND
Release date: 8 May
Catalogue number: uncomfirmed
CD1: Coming Around; Just The Faces Change; The Connection
CD2: Coming Around; The Weight (Live on *Later*);
Slide Show Video

ALBUMS

GOOD FEELING
Release date: 8 September 1997
Catalogue number: ISOM 1CD
Highest Chart Position: 9
All I Want To Do Is Rock; U16 Girls; The Line is Fine;
Good Day to Die; Good Feeling; Midsummer Nights Dreamin';
Tied to the 90's; I Love You Anyways; Happy; More Than Us;
Falling Down; Funny Thing

THE MAN WHO
Release date: 24 May 1999
Highest Chart Position: 1
Writing to Reach You; The Fear; As You Are;
Driftwood; The Last Laugh of the Laughter; Turn;
Why Does It Always Rain On Me?; Luv; She's So Strange;
Slide Show; Blue Flashing Light (hidden track)

NEW from

INDEPENDENT MUSIC PRESS

NEW FICTION FROM BRITAIN'S MOST ROCK 'N' ROLL LABEL

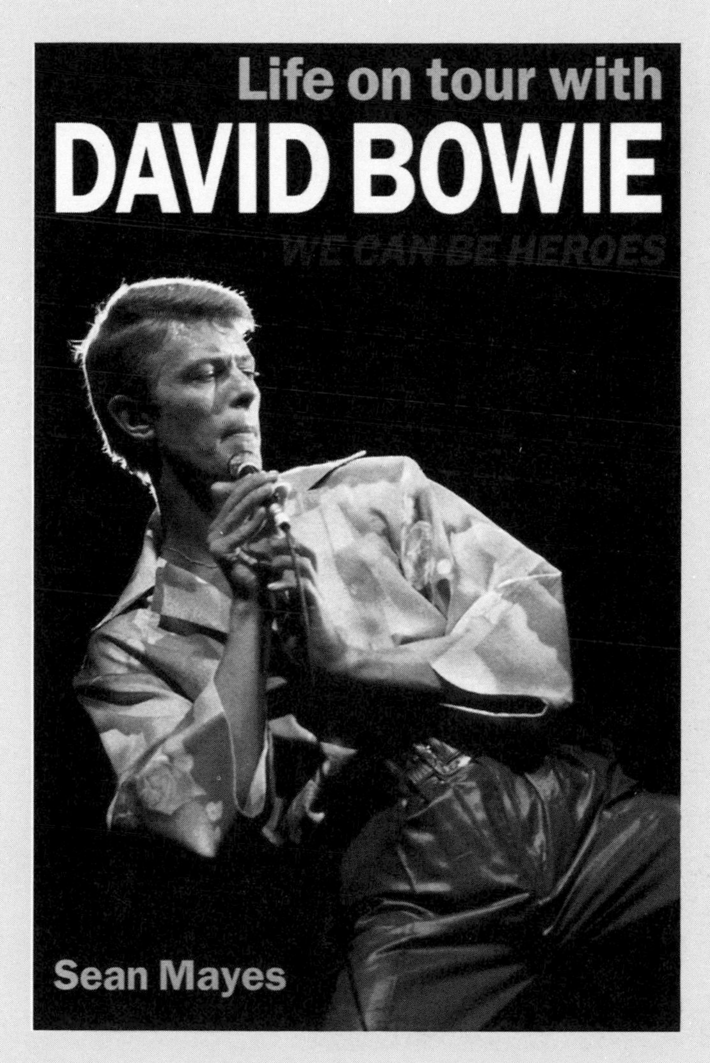

LIFE ON TOUR WITH DAVID BOWIE - WE CAN BE HEROES

In 1978, Sean Mayes toured the world with David Bowie. Travelling first class and performing each night with one of the world's greatest rock stars at the height of his fame was an amazing experience - fortunately, Sean had the foresight to document it.

Here for the first time in complete book form, Sean's tour diary is presented; a blow by blow record of how it felt to be part of a real rock circus, from rehearsals in Dallas through shows across the US, UK, Europe, Australasia and Japan to recording in London and Switzerland.

Providing page after page of fascinating insights into life on the road with Bowie, Sean's account is a unique travelogue, a must for any Bowie fan or, indeed, anyone interested in life on a sell-out world tour.

Also includes a full tour chronology and previously unpublished photos from Sean's personal archive.

By Sean Mayes
160 pages
£7.99 + £1.00p+p

to order any of these books:
PLEASE MAKE CHEQUES/POSTAL ORDERS, INTERNATIONAL MONEY ORDERS PAYABLE TO:
INDEPENDENT MUSIC PRESS LTD.

and send your payments to:
I. M. P., P.O.BOX 14691, LONDON SE1 3ZJ

Please allow 14 days for delivery

NEW from

I INDEPENDENT MUSIC PRESS 

BRITAIN'S LEADING ALTERNATIVE MUSIC PUBLISHER

IAN MCCULLOCH - KING OF COOL

Ian McCulloch was born with the gift of a golden voice. He was the Bowie freak who dreamed of rock stardom and found it as the outspoken leader of Echo And The Bunnymen, arguably the most brilliant and bewildering band in recent pop history.

For ten years it was a feast of rock 'n' roll hedonism. Then, as McCulloch's self-confessed ego became increasingly bloated, the band imploded. Against the odds, Echo And The Bunnymen were to return triumphantly in the late nineties as unlikely godfathers to an entire generation of post-Britpop contenders.

By Mick Middles
208pgs including 8pgs b/w plates
£9.99 + £1.00p+p

RHYMING & STEALING: A HISTORY OF THE BEASTIE BOYS

The first biographical attempt to document the band's metamorphosis from their initial incarnation as Greenwich Village punk rockers, through their days as rap's biggest pop stars and on to their present status as all-conquering multi-media coolest people in rock.

This volatile and fascinating history examines their beer-soaked rise to global infamy, the phenomenal commercial success of the Licensed To Ill album, as well as their years in the wilderness and the criticalrehabilitation afforded to them during the Ill Communication period.

With comprehensive accounts of the band's entire career, including their many side-projects such as the Grand Royale label, their magazine and clothing range, as well as their championing of the Tibetan Freedom cause, Rhyming & Stealing is the first full history of one of modern music's most important and influential bands.

By Angus Batey
208pgs including 8pgs b/w plates
£9.99 + £1.00p+p

PRODIGY - THE FAT OF THE LAND

The official book to accompany the global No. 1 album. The Prodigy are the world's biggest selling hard dance act - with over five million records sold and Top Ten singles in over thirty countries, they are both internationally successful and critically revered. This official book reveals, in entirely the band's own words, the thinking behind such ground-breaking releases as 'Firestarter' and 'Breathe', and gives an insider's view on their remarkable live show and life in The Prodigy.

With dozens of unpublished colour and duotone shots of the band backstage, live, in the studio and at home, The Fat Of The Land is a unique and essential visual insight into The Prodigy, as well as a stunning snapshot of a band that have single-handedly redefined modern music.

By Martin Roach
112pgs
£12.99 + £1.50p+p

SHAUN RYDER: HAPPY MONDAYS, BLACK GRAPE & OTHER TRAUMAS

Formed from the fringes of juvenile criminality in Swinton in 1984, Happy Mondays established themselves, not so much as a band in the traditional sense, but as a swirling vortex of wild hedonism. Fuelled by endless tales of petty thievery, drug dealing, pill popping, skag smoking, car smashing, purse nabbing, liberty taking and rogue-ish near anarchy, Happy Mondays careered uncontrollably through the heart of the late eighties Madchester rave scene before finally imploding in spectacular fashion.

This book chronicles this story and details how, from the ashes of the Mondays, self-confessed heroin addict and ex-postman, Shaun Ryder defied all the odds to emerge triumphant as the front man of Black Grape, arguably the only band who fulfilled the potential laid down by their flawed predecessors.

By Mick Middles
208pgs including 8pgs b/w plates
£9.99 + £1.00p+p

DIARY OF A ROCK 'N' ROLL STAR - IAN HUNTER

Widely regarded as the first rock autobiography and universally acclaimed as one of the finest ever insights into life on the road, this best-selling title is now re-printed for the first time in 15 years. Revealing the rigours of Mott The Hoople's enigmatic frontman, this is a landmark publication. Q magazine simply called it "the greatest music book ever written."

By Ian Hunter
160pgs with 28 photo's
£8.95 + £1.00p+p

OASIS - ROUND THEIR WAY
This is the first major biography of Oasis, the multi-million selling Manchester band led by the Gallagher brothers Noel and Liam.

Round Their Way follows the Oasis story from their unlikely beginnings as The Rain to their present day status as the most talked about band in the world. Includes full details of the sibling rivalry between Noel and Liam, their family life in Manchester, their infamous rock 'n' roll reputation, and includes the most comprehensive Oasis discography ever published.

By Mick Middles
128pgs including 8pgs b/w
£9.99 + £1.00p+p

POP BOOK NUMBER ONE - STEVE GULLICK
This fine collection of Steve Gullick's work from 1988-1995 captures the key figures in alternative world music. With rare and unpublished shots of Nirvana, Pearl Jam, Hole, Blur, Bjork, and many more, this is the most accomplished photo history of alternative music. *The Times* called it "one of the most beautiful and necessary books about 1990's pop and rock" whilst *Melody Maker* said "So stylish, so rockin'."

By Steve Gullick
112pgs with 108 duo-tone photo's
£12.95 + £1.50p+p

THE BUZZCOCKS - THE COMPLETE HISTORY
The fully authorised biography of one of the prime movers of the original punk scene. Author Tony McGartland recounts in stunning detail every gig, rehearsal, tour, record release and studio session the band ever played, and reveals rare unpublished photo's. *Record Collector* said "this book is invaluable", *Vox* called it "a bible for Buzzcocks fans" whilst *Q* declared it to be "an exhaustive documentation of these punk pop perfecto's that only prime mover Pete Shelley could possibly improve upon."

By Tony McGartland
160pgs with 25 photo's
£8.95 + £1.25p+p

THE PRODIGY - ELECTRONIC PUNKS
The official history of the world's most successful hard dance band, including hours of exclusive interviews with band members, families and friends, as well as photographs taken almost entirely from the band's own personal albums. *Electronic Punks* moved *NME* to call Martin Roach "the biographer of alternative Britain."

By Martin Roach
160pgs with 38 photo's
£5.99 + £1.00p+p

MEGA CITY FOUR: TALL STORIES & CREEPY CRAWLIES
This authorised biography is a comprehensive study of of this seminal band, containing 40 photographs taken from the band's own album, over 30 hours of interviews and a complete discography. *NME* said "its attention to detail is stunning", *Q* magazine said "the incredible detail is breathtaking", whilst *Record Collector* hailed it as "a valuable account, true drama."

By Martin Roach
208pgs with 40 photo's
£6.99 + £1.00p+p

THE RIGHT TO IMAGINATION AND MADNESS
With an Introduction by John Peel. This landmark book provides lengthy interviews with 20 of the UK's top alternative songwriters including Johnny Marr, Ian McCulloch, Billy Bragg, Prodigy, Boo Radleys, The The, Pwei, MC4, Napalm Death, Wedding Present, Senseless Things, Utah Saints, BTTP, Aphex Twin, McNabb, Ride.

By Martin Roach
450pgs with 35 photo's
£9.99 + £1.25p+p

THE MISSION: NAMES ARE FOR TOMBSTONES, BABY
The official and fully authorised biography of one of the UK's biggest goth bands. *Melody Maker* said "This makes Hammer of the Gods look like a Cliff Richard biog!", *The Times* praised the "impressively detailed research" whilst *Record Collector* hailed "a tight fluid book which pulls no punches with an enviable degree of confidence, all utterly compelling stuff."

By Martin Roach
288pgs with 38 photo's
£6.99 + £1.00p+p

THE EIGHT LEGGED ATOMIC DUSTBIN WILL EAT ITSELF
The first and only detailed account of Stourbridge's finest, including previously unpublished photographs, exclusive interviews, a complete discography and reviewography, and an introduction by Clint Poppie. *Vox* described the debut book and its success as "phenomenal".

By Martin Roach
160pgs with 38 photo's
£6.99 + £1.00p+p

How to order any of these books:
PLEASE MAKE CHEQUES/POSTAL ORDERS, INTERNATIONAL MONEY ORDERS PAYABLE TO:
INDEPENDENT MUSIC PRESS LTD.

and send your payments to:
I. M. P., P.O.BOX 14691, LONDON SE1 3ZJ

Please allow 14 days for delivery

also available from

I.M.P. FICTION

NALDA SAID

An intriguing debut novel from the bass player for Belle & Sebastian and Looper

Riddled by an intense fear of his bizarre secret being discovered, the narrator of *Nalda Said* grows up in the strange seclusion of a shoddy caravan with his Aunt Nalda, whose own colourful storytelling leaves him perpetually trapped between fantasy and reality.

Nalda's nephew eventually finds work as a hospital gardener where, perhaps for the first time, he finds true friendship and begins to realise that his dark secret has been suffocating what hope he had of ever leading a normal life.

Finding himself in love, this socially disjointed figure struggles to reconcile his own curious view of the world with the stark daily reality that most people are forced to live with. Yet, his own bleak battle to break free from these mental shackles oddly reflects the desperation of the very same people who cruelly poke fun at him.

Nalda Said is a disturbing, compelling and brilliantly crafted tale of one man's pained anxiety and desperate search for his dream - to live a normal life.

Stuart David *is frontman of* ***LOOPER****, the unique Glaswegian band hailed by the NME as "a gentle act of madness." Their debut album "Up A Tree" was declared one of the New Yorker magazine's 12 Favorite CD's of 1999.*

By Stuart David
160 pages
£7.99 + £1.00p+p

...low to order any of these books:

PLEASE MA... HEQUES ... L ORDERS, INTERNATIONAL MONEY ORDERS PAYABLE TO:

...PENDENT MUSIC PRESS LTD.

and send your payments to:

I. M... P.O.BOX 14691, LONDON SE1 3ZJ

Please allow 14 days for delivery